THE
LIBRARY COPYRIGHT
GUIDE

COPYRIGHT INFORMATION BULLETIN SERIES

1. Jerome K. Miller, *Using Copyrighted Videocassettes in Classrooms and Libraries*, 1984 (out of print).

2. Charles W. Vlcek, *Copyright Policy Development: A Resource Book for Educators*, 1987.

3. Jerome K. Miller, *Using Copyrighted Videocassettes in Classrooms, Libraries, and Training Centers*, 2d. ed., 1987.

4. Esther R. Sinofsky, *A Copyright Primer for Educational and Industrial Media Producers*, 1988.

5. Jerome K. Miller (Ed.), *Video Copyright Permissions: A Guide to Securing Permission to Retain, Perform, and Transmit Television Programs Videotaped Off the Air*, 1989.

6. Charles W. Vlcek, *Adoptable Copyright Policy: Copyright Policy and Manuals Designed For Adoption By Schools, Colleges & Universities*, 1992.

7. Leonard DuBoff, *High-Tech Law (In Plain English)*® : An Entrepreneur's Guide, 1991.

8. Ruth H. Dukelow, *The Library Copyright Guide*, 1992.

THE
LIBRARY COPYRIGHT
GUIDE

By

Ruth H. Dukelow

COPYRIGHT INFORMATION SERVICES

COPYRIGHT INFORMATION SERVICES

An imprint of the
Association for Educational Communications and Technology
1025 Vermont Ave., NW, Suite 820, Washington, DC 20005

ISBN 0-89240-067-6

Printed in the United States of America by
BookCrafters, Chelsea, Michigan

Typeset at AAH Graphics, Seven Fountains, Virginia

The Association for Educational Communications and Technology is an international professional association dedicated to the improvement of instruction through the effective use of media and technology. Periodicals, monographs, videotapes and audiotapes available through AECT meet the needs of media and learning resource specialists, educators, librarians, industrial trainers, and a variety of other educational technology professionals.

DEDICATION

For my parents
Owen and Harriet

DISCLAIMER

The opinions contained herein
reflect the author's informed opinions
but do not constitute legal advice.

TABLE OF CONTENTS

PREFACE

The Library Copyright Guide is written to help librarians comply with the Copyright Act of 1976 when duplicating copyrighted materials. Permissible levels of duplication vary depending on whether the reproductions are made for patrons, for interlibrary loan, or for internal use. This single source contains background information, guidelines, statutory references, and other interpretive materials relating to the library and archives exemption to the exclusive right of reproduction, established in section 108 of the Copyright Revision Act of 1976. This book covers the history of section 108 and analyzes each part of section 108. It also includes a chapter on acquiring permission to duplicate materials when the copying does not fall under the protection of section 108.

This book emphasizes permissible duplication under section 108 and does not attempt to explain in detail section 107 on "fair use." Fair use is discussed briefly in Chapter Seven insofar as the library or archives may be called upon by users (e.g., faculty) to make such copies on library equipment. An indepth study of fair use is not presented here as it would require another book the size of this one.

This book also includes a brief explanation of exclusive performance rights. This subject is treated briefly in Chapter Eight to introduce librarians to this complex body of law, particularly as it applies to film, video, and live performances in libraries. Many other aspects of performance rights are omitted.

Ruth H. Dukelow, J.D., M.S.L.S.
Lansing, Michigan
1992

PART I:

THE SECTION 108 EXEMPTION FOR LIBRARY REPRODUCTION OF COPYRIGHTED MATERIALS

Chapter 1

HISTORY OF SECTION 108

The U.S. Congress which existed under the Articles of Confederation had no authority over copyrights. Because of the problems authors faced in protecting their rights, the Congress recommended that the States pass acts securing copyright for fourteen years. By 1786, Connecticut, Massachusetts, Virginia, New York, and New Jersey had all passed copyright acts and others were considering them, much due to the efforts of Noah Webster's crusade encouraging copyright acts.[1]

The Constitutional Congress first addressed nationwide copyright protection in 1789 in the United States Constitution, Article I, Section 1, clause 8, which provides "To promote the Progress of Science and useful Arts, by securing for limited Times to Authors and Inventors the exclusive Right to their Writings and Discoveries."[2]

The Constitutional provision for copyright protection was accepted without controversy. At its first session in 1789, Congress passed the first copyright law. The law has been amended many times and completely revised four times.[3] The most recent complete revision is the Copyright Act of 1976, effective January 1, 1978. The 1976 Act was

---

1   Putnam, George Haven, comp., *The question of copyright* (New York: Putnam, 1891), p. 102.

2   U.S. Const., Art. 1, Sec. 1, cl. 8. These exclusive rights (which include the right of reproduction) are enumerated in section 106 of the Copyright Act of 1976, 17 U.S.C. 106, and are discussed in detail in Chapter 2.

3   1831, 1870, 1909, and 1976.

3

the first to provide a limited exemption for reproduction of copyrighted materials by libraries and archives.[4]

Prior to the 1976 Act, the copyright laws did not directly address the issue of library copying of copyrighted materials, and libraries had only "fair use" caselaw to help them determine whether their duplication of copyrighted materials was permissible. Since none of the cases involved libraries, this determination was often difficult. To assist libraries and archives in this matter, a "Gentlemen's Agreement" was devised in 1935. Until the 1960's, it was assumed that the judicial concept of fair use had some application to library photocopying. This assumption was challenged, however, when the *Williams & Wilkins*[5] case (which was filed in 1968 and received its final decision in 1975) took the issue of library photocopying to court.

Section 108 of the 1976 Act, the limited exemption for libraries and archives, had its beginnings in the "Gentlemen's Agreement" and in the *Williams & Wilkins* case. Section 108 also is the product of prolonged negotiations between publishers and librarians leading to the copyright revision act to replace the 1909 Act. This Chapter examines the "Gentlemen's Agreement," the *Williams & Wilkins* case, and the legislative development of section 108, all of which contributed to the adoption of the library and archives exemption to the right of reproduction.

THE GENTLEMEN'S AGREEMENT OF 1935

The complete revision of the copyright law in 1909 did not address the issue of a library's or archives' duplication of copyrighted materials. In the 1930's, when "photographic reprography" was introduced, publishers became concerned that their copyrighted materials would lose their pecuniary value, due to uncontrolled duplication by libraries and archives. To address this concern, the "Gentlemen's Agreement" was entered into by representatives from the National Association of Book Publishers and a Joint Committee on Materials for Research of the Amer-

---

4   17 U.S.C. 108.
5   *Williams & Wilkins Co. v. United States.* 172 U.S.P.Q. 670 (Comm'r Ct. Cl. 1973), *rev'd* 487 F.2d 1345 (Ct.Cl. 1973), *aff'd by an equally-divided court,* 420 U.S. 376 (1975).

ican Council of Learned Societies and the Social Science Research Council.

Under this Agreement, a library or archives office could make a single reproduction of part of a copyrighted work, as follows:

> A library, archives office, museum, or similar institution owning books or periodical volumes in which copyright still subsists may make and deliver a single photographic reproduction or reduction of a part thereof to a scholar representing in writing that he desires such reproduction in lieu of loan of such publication or in place of manual transcription and solely for the purposes of research; provided
>
> (1) That the person receiving it is given due notice in writing that he is not exempt from liability to the copyright proprietor for any infringement of copyright by misuse of the reproduction constituting an infringement under the copyright law;
>
> (2) That such reproduction is made and furnished without profit to itself by the institution making it.
>
> The exemption from liability of the library, archives office or museum herein provided for shall extend to every officer, agent or employee of such institution in the making and delivery of such reproduction when acting within the scope of his authority of employment. This exemption for the institution itself carries with it a responsibility to see that library employees caution patrons against the misuse of copyright material reproduced photographically.[6]

The "Gentlemen's Agreement" was useful for a time[7], but it did not offer a complete solution, as interlibrary loan was not addressed by the Agreement. As the Register of Copyrights notes,

> The approach of the 1935 Agreement is toward a limited copying arrangement enjoyed by libraries by virtue of their ownership of the physical materials from which they copy for users. The era of national and regional bibliographic data bases,

---

6   "The Gentlemen's Agreement and the problem of copyright," *Journal of Documentary Reproduction* 2 (1939): 31–32. See Appendix 1 for complete text of the Agreement.
7   When the National Assn. of Book Publishers folded, its successor, the Assn. of American Publishers, repudiated the Gentlemen's Agreement.

huge populations of students and specialized researchers, co-ordinated collection development and "ILL" then lay in the future and, of course, was not provided for.[8]

Although the Agreement was somewhat satisfactory at its inception, technological changes and the changing needs of researchers and other library users quickly rendered the document obsolete. As early as the 1950's,[9] Congress began to consider revising the 1909 Act to address the publishers' concerns with the rapid advancement of photo-duplication technology and the librarians' concerns with serving the changing needs of their users. Congress' copyright revision efforts did not move quickly enough for some publishers. In 1968 a publisher of medical journals, the Williams & Wilkins Co., brought a lawsuit challenging the photocopying practices of the National Library of Medicine and the library of the National Institutes of Health.[10]

WILLIAMS & WILKINS CO. V. UNITED STATES

Plaintiff Williams & Wilkins Co., a publisher of thirty-seven medical books, brought a copyright infringement action against the United States for making unauthorized photocopies. Williams & Wilkins Co. charged that the Department of Health, Education, and Welfare, through the National Institutes of Health (NIH) and the National Library of Medicine (NLM), made unauthorized photocopies from four of the company's journals: *Medicine, Journal of Immunology, Gastroenterology*, and *Pharmacological Reviews*.[11] Eight specific articles were at issue and were shown to have been copied at the request of NIH researchers and an Army medical officer in connection with their professional work.[12]

---

8 U.S. Library of Congress, Copyright Office, *Report of the Register of Copyrights: Library reproduction of copyrighted works* (17 U.S.C. 108). (Washington, DC: January 1983), p. 15.

9 *Copyright law revision studies pursuant to S. Res. 240, 86th Cong., 2nd Sess.* (Comm. Print. 1960). See specifically: A. Doyle, et al., *Notice of copyright, study no. 7*; A. Latman, *Fair use of copyrighted works, study no 14*; B. Varmer, *Photoduplication of copyrighted materials by libraries, study no. 15.*

10 Williams & Wilkins Co. was urged by AAP and other publishers not to file the suit and to wait for the revision act. The other publishers did not join the suit until Williams & Wilkins Co. was financially unable to fund an appeal.

11 *Williams & Wilkins Co. v. U.S.*, 487 F.2d 1345, 1347 (Ct. Cl. 1973).

12 487 F.2d 1345, 1349.

Although this case concerned only eight specific articles, evidence showed that both NIH and NLM regularly photocopied voluminous numbers of journal articles. In representative years, NIH supplied copies of approximately 93,000 articles (1970)[13] and NLM provided copies of 120,000 articles (1968).[14] This duplication was limited only by the agencies' policies to prevent excessive copying. The NIH library's policy stated that only a single copy of a journal article would be made per request (which was limited to about forty to fifty pages) and that, with some exceptions, the library would copy only a single article from a journal issue.[15] NLM's policy similarly stated that it would provide only one photocopy of a particular article per request and that it would not photocopy an entire journal issue.[16] NLM's policy also limited the number of requests per month from an individual (maximum of twenty) or institution (maximum of thirty) with the restriction of no more than one article from a single journal issue and no more than three from a journal volume.[17]

The trial court held that the Government was liable for infringement of copyright. On review, the Court of Claims reversed and held that the United States was free of liability in this case.[18] The Court of Claims, however, underscored the need for legislation on library photocopying, stating:

> The 1909 Act gives almost nothing by way of directives, the judicial doctrine of "fair use" is amorphous and open-ended, and the courts are now precluded, both by the Act and by the nature of the judicial process, from contriving pragmatic or compromise solutions which would reflect the legislature's choices of policy and its mediation among the competing interests. The Supreme Court has pointed out that such a "job is for Congress." . . . Hopefully, the result in the present case will be but a "holding operation" in the interim period before Congress enacts its preferred solution.[19]

---

13   487 F.2d 1345, 1348.
14   487 F.2d 1345, 1349.
15   487 F.2d 1345, 1348.
16   487 F.2d 1345, 1348.
17   487 F.2d 1345, 1349.
18   487 F.2d 1345, 1347.
19   487 F.2d 1345, 1363.

7

The U.S. Supreme Court affirmed the Court of Claims' decision by a divided (four-four) Court, with Justice Blackmun abstaining.[20]This decision clearly indicated that, as the Court of Claims suggested, it was up to Congress to provide a solution to the problem of photocopying copyrighted materials, especially those retained in library collections.

COMMITTEE REPORTS ON SECTION 108

During the courts' prolonged deliberation of the *Williams & Wilkins* case (1968-1975), Congress sought a legislative solution to the problems presented by photocopying technology and the special needs of libraries and archives. The library and archives exemption to the exclusive right of reproduction emerged through a series of House and Senate Committee Reports: H.R. Rep. No. 2237 (10/12/66), H.R. Rep. No. 83 (3/8/67), Sen. Rep. No. 473 (11/20/75), H.R. Rep. No. 1476 (9/3/76), and H.R. Rep. No. 1733 (Conference, 9/29/76).[21]

H.R. Rep. No. 2237

In 1966, the House Committee on the Judiciary said it did not "favor special fair use provisions dealing with the problems of library photocopying" but saw a need for "a specific exemption permitting reproduction of manuscript collections under certain conditions."[22] In response to a request from representatives of archivists and historians, the Committee developed an archival reproduction privilege, section 108, which provided:

> Nonprofit institutions having archival custody over manuscripts or similar collections of unpublished works of scholarly value are given the privilege of making facsimile reproductions of works in their collections, as long as the reproduction is not done for profit and is for purposes of preservation and security, or for deposit for research use in another institution of the same type.[23]

---

20 *Williams & Wilkins Co. v. U.S.*, 420 U.S. 376 (1975).
21 Portions of these Reports relevant to section 108 are reproduced in Appendices 5, 6, 7, and 8.
22 H.R. Rep. No. 2237, 89th Cong., 2d Sess. (1966).
23 H.R. Rep. No. 2237, p. 33–34.

The Report stated specifically that copies were not to be distributed to scholars or the public.[24]

H.R. Rep. No. 83

In 1967, the House Committee on the Judiciary repeated verbatim the section 108 commentary of H.R. Rep. No. 2237.

Sen. Rep. No. 473

In 1975, the Senate Committee on the Judiciary proposed a greatly expanded section 108 which provided for libraries and archives to provide single photocopies to users under limited circumstances. The revised version of section 108 provided for archival reproduction, replacement of damaged copies, duplication of articles and small excerpts, copying out-of-print works, and other general exemptions.[25] An interesting special exemption for audiovisual news programs was added specifically to protect the Vanderbilt University Television News Archive in its copyright infringement suit with CBS News.[26]

The proposed section 108 excluded musical works, pictorial, graphic, and sculptural works, and motion pictures and other audiovisual works from its coverage and also contained prohibitions against multiple copies and systematic reproduction.[27] "Systematic" reproduction was defined quite narrowly and would have greatly restricted interlibrary loan and other library photocopying arrangements.[28]

H.R. Rep. No. 1476

The September 3, 1976, Report of the House Committee on the Judiciary expanded upon the comments of the previous Senate Report and focused on the determination of which libraries and archives are qualified for the exemption, stating that a purely commercial enterprise could not "establish a collection of copyrighted works, call itself a li-

---

24 H.R. Rep. No. 2237, p. 67.
25 Sen. Rep. No. 473, 94th Cong., 1st Sess. (1975), pp. 67–69.
26 Sen. Rep. No. 473, p. 69. For a more detailed discussion of the audiovisual news program exemption, see Chapter 4.
27 Sen. Rep. No. 473, p. 70–71.
28 Sen. Rep. No. 473, p. 70–71.

brary or archive, and engage in for-profit reproduction and distribution of photocopies."[29]

This Report also revised the Senate's proposed provisions on "systematic" copying to clarify that certain interlibrary loan arrangements would not be considered "systematic" if the duplication was not performed "in such aggregate quantities as to substitute for a subscription to or purchase of such work."[30]

Some publishers and others were fearful that the new, untried exemption would not provide a proper balance between the rights of copyright holders and users. Although section 108 looked reasonable on paper, its actual working effect was unknown. In response to those concerns, the House Committee also added a new subsection (i) requiring the Register of Copyrights to review section 108 at five-year intervals.

H.R. Rep. No. 1733.

The Conference Committee, which was formed to reconcile the differences between the House and Senate versions of the proposed Copyright Act, issued its Report on September 29, 1976. In regard to section 108, the Conference adopted the House provisions relating to "systematic" copying and set forth specific guidelines for interlibrary loan photocopying arrangements as proposed by the National Commission on New Technological Uses of Copyrighted Works (the CONTU guidelines).[31] This final version was adopted by Congress and was enacted as part of the Copyright Revision Act of 1976, effective January 1, 1978.

FIVE-YEAR REPORT OF THE REGISTER OF COPYRIGHTS

The Copyright Act of 1976 requires the Register of Copyrights to issue a report every five years on section 108:

---

29 H.R. Rep. No. 1476, 94th Cong., 2d Sess. (1976). For a more detailed discussion of which libraries and archives are eligible for the section 108 exemption, see Chapter 3.

30 H.R. Rep. No. 1476, p. 78.

31 H.R. Rep. No. 1733, 94th Cong., 2d Sess. (1976), pp. 70–74. For a more detailed discussion of the CONTU guidelines, see Chapter 6.

(i) Five years from the effective date of this Act, and at five-year intervals thereafter, the Register of Copyrights, after consulting with representatives of authors, book and periodical publishers, and other owners of copyrighted materials, and with representatives of library users and librarians, shall submit to the Congress a report setting forth the extent to which this section has achieved the intended statutory balancing of the rights of creators, and the needs of users. The report should also describe any problems that may have arisen, and present legislative or other recommendations, if warranted.[32]

The first Report was issued in January 1983 and was quite critical of library and archival practices. The second, which was issued in January 1988, was more favorable. Both Reports include recommendations for certain guidelines and statutory clarifications, but in general, section 108 is accepted as a workable solution to the problem of libraries' and archives' duplication of copyrighted materials. As the Register of Copyrights notes in the latest five-year review:

> Most of the major library associations (the American Library Association, the Association of Research Libraries, the Special Libraries Association, and the Medical Library Association) stated that Congress has achieved a statutory balance. Representatives of proprietors (the American Association of Publishers, Harcourt Brace Jovanovich and The Authors League of America) also joined in the view that a reasonable balance between the competing interests had been struck in the statutory formation of 108.[33]

SUMMARY

The U.S. Constitution, Article I, Section 1, clause 8, authorized Congress to pass laws providing copyright protection for a limited time to authors for their works. This protection includes the copyright owner's exclusive right to reproduce copies. Prior to the adoption of section 108 of the Copyright Act of 1976, there was no statutory provision to address

---

32 17 U.S.C. 108(i).
33 U.S. Library of Congress, Copyright Office, *Report of the Register of Copyrights; Library reproduction of copyrighted works* (17 U.S.C. 108) (Washington, DC: January, 1988), p. 118.

11

the problem of photocopying copyrighted materials owned by libraries and archives.

The Gentlemen's Agreement of 1935, executed by representatives from publishers, scholars, libraries, and archives, attempted to reach a workable arrangement whereby scholars could make single copies of copyrighted materials for personal research. This Agreement was made obsolete by rapid technological advances and by the changing needs of library users.

In the 1968 case of *Williams & Wilkins Co. v. U.S.*, the plaintiff publishing company brought a copyright infringement suit against NIH and NLM for making unauthorized copies of some of its journal articles. The Court of Claims narrowly held for the United States, and, in 1975, the Supreme Court affirmed the decision by an equally-divided Court (4-4).

The House and Senate Reports which make up the legislative history of section 108 show that Congress realized the special needs of library users and balanced those needs against the concerns of publishers. To ensure that section 108 continues to provide a good balance, section 108(i) of the Copyright Act of 1976 requires the Register of Copyrights to conduct five-year appraisals of section 108. The next Registrar's report is due in 1993.

Chapter 2

THE COPYRIGHT OWNER'S EXCLUSIVE RIGHTS

The Copyright Act of 1976 grants copyright owners five exclusive rights to their copyrighted materials: reproduction, adaptation, distribution, public performance, and public display. Copyright owners may choose to exercise these rights themselves, or they may give or sell all or part of the rights to others. Unauthorized use of copyrighted material is an infringement of the owner's copyright unless it is permitted under one of the exceptions to the exclusive rights.

A person wishing to use copyrighted material without infringing on the owner's exclusive rights must either:

(1) demonstrate that the proposed use does not fall under one of the five exclusive rights of section 106;

(2) demonstrate that the proposed use is a "fair use" under the section 107 "limitation on exclusive rights";

(3) demonstrate that the proposed use falls under one of the other "limitations on exclusive rights" provided under sections 108-117; or

(4) obtain written authorization from the copyright owner.

This Chapter examines briefly the five exclusive rights and introduces the library exemption for reproduction. "Fair use" and other limitations are discussed briefly in Chapters Seven and Eight. Obtaining permission from the copyright owner is covered separately in Chapter Nine.

EXCLUSIVE RIGHTS UNDER SECTION 106

Section 106 of the Copyright Act of 1976 provides that copyright owners have exclusive rights to do and to authorize any of the following:

(1) to reproduce the copyrighted work in copies or phonorecords;

(2) to prepare derivative works based upon the copyrighted work;

(3) to distribute copies or phonorecords of the copyrighted work to the public by sale of other transfer of ownership, or by rental, lease, or lending;

(4) in the case of literary, musical, dramatic, and choreographic works, pantomimes, and motion pictures and other audiovisual works, to perform the copyrighted work publicly; and

(5) in the case of literary, musical, dramatic, and choreographic works, pantomimes, and pictorial, graphic, or sculptural works, including the individual images of a motion picture or other audiovisual work, to display the copyrighted work publicly.[34]

Reproduction

The first right of section 106, the right of reproduction, reserves to the copyright owner the right to duplicate the copyrighted work in copies or phonorecords. This includes all methods of duplication, such as photocopying, videotaping, photographing, making copies of computer software, etc. The focus of this book is the section 108 limitation on this right of reproduction granted to libraries and archives.

Adaptation

The second right, the right of adaptation, reserves to the copyright owner the right to prepare derivative works from the original. For example, the copyright owner of a novel has the exclusive right to adapt the novel into a stage play, a film, an opera or musical, an epic poem,

---

34   17 U.S.C. 106.

a puppet show, a pantomime, an abridged version of the novel, or any other format or style. Fictional characters, such as Snoopy or Mickey Mouse, have been adapted to jewelry, garments, greeting cards, etc.

Distribution

The third right, the right of distribution, reserves to the copyright owner the right to transfer ownership (by sale or otherwise) of copies of the work to members of the public, or to rent, lease, or lend copies of the work. This right of distribution, often called the "right of first publication," only extends to the publication or first sale of a particular copy. If the copyright owner has transferred ownership of a copy, "the person to whom the copy . . . is transferred is entitled to dispose of it by sale, rental, or any other means."[35] In other words, barring any contractual restrictions imposed at the time of the sale, a library which has purchased a copy of a copyrighted work, in any medium, may lend it or may sell it, or otherwise transfer ownership of the copy without infringing on the copyright owner's right of distribution.

Public Performance

The fourth right, the right of public performance, was totally revised in the Copyright Revision Act of 1976. It reserves almost all public performances to the copyright owner. With some exceptions, everyone else must have permission to perform the work. This exclusive right extends to all media, including literary, musical, dramatic, and choreographic works, pantomimes, motion pictures, and other audiovisual works. "Public performances" include playing videocassettes, putting on a play, or playing a piece of music on a piano. If these works are performed in "a place open to the public or at any place where a substantial number of persons outside of a normal circle of a family or its social acquaintances is gathered,"[36] a license is usually required for the performance.

Public Display

The fifth right, the right of public display, reserves the right of most public displays to the copyright owner. This right applies to all

---

35 H.R. Rep. No. 1476, p. 79.
36 17 U.S.C. 101.

works, but has special relevance to the visual arts. For example, showing a slide in a public place would constitute "public display."

To avoid infringement, a person proposing to reproduce, adapt, distribute, perform, or display a copyrighted work must demonstrate that the proposed use is exempt under sections 107–118 of the Copyright Act of 1976. Some of these exemptions are treated in Chapters Seven and Eight.

LIBRARY AND ARCHIVAL EXEMPTION TO THE RIGHT OF REPRODUCTION

Under limited circumstances, section 108 of the Copyright Revision Act of 1976 permits libraries and archives to duplicate copyrighted materials without infringing on the copyright owner's exclusive right of reproduction.[37] Chapters Three through Six of this book cover in detail the components of the section 108 limitation, including which libraries and archives are granted the exemption, the amount of material which may be copied and for what purposes, and other considerations.

Section 108 provides a separate and distinct exemption to the exclusive right of reproduction which should not be confused with "fair use" or other limitations on exclusive rights. See Chapters Seven and Eight for a brief discussion of "fair use" and other exemptions.

SUMMARY

Copyright owners are granted five exclusive rights to their works: the right of reproduction, the right of adaptation, the right of distribution, the right of public performance, and the right of public display. Unauthorized use of a copyrighted work involving any of these five rights is an infringement of copyright unless the use falls within one of the "limitations on exclusive rights" set forth in sections 107-117 of the Copyright Act of 1976.

Section 108 provides that, under limited circumstances, libraries and archives may duplicate copyrighted materials without infringing on the copyright owner's exclusive right of reproduction. See Chapters Three through Six for a thorough examination of this limitation.

---

37 17 U.S.C. 108.

Chapter 3

ELIGIBILITY FOR EXEMPTION UNDER SECTION 108

Section 108 of the Copyright Act of 1976, "Limitations on exclusive rights: Reproduction by libraries and archives," allows limited photo-copying of copyrighted works by libraries and archives. This section, which did not appear in the former 1909 law, was added to provide a balance between the copyright holder's rights and the user's needs, "in a way both consistent with traditional principles of copyright law and library practice and not exceeding a minimal encroachment upon the rights of authors and copyright owners."[38]

Under Section 108(a), photocopying by libraries and archives is not an infringement if the copying meets three criteria:

(1) the reproduction or distribution is made without any purpose of direct or indirect commercial advantage;

(2) the collections of the library or archives are (i) open to the public, or (ii) available not only to researchers affiliated with the library or archives or with the institutions of which it is a part, but also to other persons doing research in a specialized field; and

(3) the reproduction or distribution of the work includes a notice of copyright.[39]

All three of the above criteria must be met for a use to be permitted

---

38 *Report of the Register of Copyrights* (January, 1983), p. vii.
39 17 U.S.C. 108(a).

under Section 108. If the photocopying of a certain item fails to meet any of these three criteria, then that use would not be protected by Section 108. A use not covered by Section 108 might, of course, fall under the "fair use" provisions of copyright law, and the user would then be required to show compliance with the criteria listed in Section 107.

No Direct or Indirect Commercial Advantage

Section 108(a)(1) provides that reproduction or distribution must be made "without any purpose of direct or indirect commercial advantage." At first glance, the language of this provision appears to indicate that the library or archives must not profit financially when charging users fees for photocopying services. The Senate and House Reports, however, give somewhat broader, and differing, viewpoints on the interpretation of Section 108(a)(1).

The Senate Report states:

> The limitation of section 108 to reproduction and distribution by libraries and archives "without any purpose of direct or indirect commercial advantage" is intended to preclude a library or archives in a profitmaking organization from providing photocopies of copyrighted materials to employees engaged in furtherance of the organization's commercial enterprise, unless such copying qualifies as a fair use, or the organization has obtained the necessary copyright licenses. A commercial organization should purchase the number of copies of a work that it requires, or obtain the consent of the copyright owner to the making of the photocopies.[40]

On the other hand, the House Report provides a different interpretation, stating that under Section 108(a)(1):

> . . . a purely commercial enterprise could not establish a collection of copyrighted works, call itself a library or archive, and engage in for-profit reproduction and distribution of photocopies. Similarly, it would not be possible for a non-profit institution, by means of contractual arrangements with a commercial copying enterprise, to authorize the enterprise to carry out copying and distribution functions that would be exempt if conducted by the non-profit institution itself.

---

40   Sen. Rep. No. 473, p. 67.

. . . .

Isolated, spontaneous making of single photocopies by a library in a for-profit organization, without any systematic effort to substitute photocopying for subscriptions or purchases, would be covered by section 108, even though the copies are furnished to the employees of the organization for use in their work. Similarly, for-profit libraries could participate in interlibrary arrangements for exchange of photocopies, as long as the production or distribution was not "systematic." These activities, by themselves, would ordinarily not be considered "for direct or indirect commercial advantages," since the "advantage" referred to in this clause must attach to the immediate commercial motivation behind the reproduction or distribution itself, rather than to the ultimate profit-making motivation behind the enterprise in which the library is located. On the other hand, section 108 would not excuse reproduction or distribution if there were a commercial motive behind the actual making or distributing of the copies, if multiple copies were made or distributed, or if the photocopying activities were "systematic" in the sense that their aim was to substitute for subscriptions or purchases.[41]

In further discussion of the issue, the Conference Report states:

Another point of interpretation involves the meaning of "indirect commercial advantage," as used in section 108(a)(1), in the case of libraries or archival collections within industrial, profit-making, or proprietary institutions. As long as the library or archives meets the criteria of section 108(a) and the other requirements of the section, including the prohibitions against multiple and systematic copying in subsection (g), the conferees consider that the isolated, spontaneous making of single photocopies by a library or archives in a for-profit organization without any commercial motivation, or participation by such library or archives in interlibrary arrangements, would come within the scope of section 108.[42]

Although we cannot predict how a court would define the limits of "direct or indirect commercial advantage," we can suggest the fol-

---

41 H.R. Rep. No. 1476, p. 74–75.
42 H.R. Rep. No. 1733, p. 73–74.

lowing guidelines to determine whether a particular use falls within the protection of Section 108(a)(1):

1. A non-profit library or archives may not contract with a for-profit enterprise to provide and distribute photocopies, unless the photocopying in question is covered by the "fair use" provisions of Section 107 or unless permission has been granted by the copyright holder. For example, a non-profit library could not contract with a commercial firm to make photocopies to fill the library's interlibrary loan requests and still fall under the protection of section 108. The extent of this ban on use of a commercial firm to provide photocopying services is unclear, however, in the situation of a library making a copy pursuant to Section 108(c) (see Chapter Four for a detailed description of this section). It would seem unreasonable for Section 108 to require that the library making an "archival" copy under Section 108(c) be required to duplicate it on library equipment, especially if the copy is a microfilm or fiche.

2. For-profit institutions may not call themselves "libraries" or "archives" and then engage in for-profit reproduction and distribution of photocopies of works protected by copyright.

3. Although there is some discrepancy between the Senate Report and the House Reports, it is likely that a for-profit institution may furnish isolated, spontaneous, single photocopies to employees of the organization for use in their work. If photocopying of a certain title becomes so frequent as to qualify as "systematic," however, the institution should purchase additional copies of the title or should obtain written permission from the copyright holder.

4. Libraries and archives in for-profit institutions may participate in interlibrary loan arrangements as long as the photocopying does not become "systematic." Also, the for-profit institution must not profit financially from the interlibrary loan functions of its library or archives.

Open or Available to the Public

Section 108(a)(2) states:

> the collections of the library or archives are (i) open to the public, or (ii) available not only to researchers affiliated with the library or archives or with the institution of which it

is a part, but also to other persons doing research in a specialized field. . .[43]

This provision requires that the collections of the library or archives be open or available, not just the physical facility where the materials are housed. These collections must either be (i) open to the public or (ii) available to researchers.

The "open to the public" requirement is met if any member of the public may use the collections of the library or archives. The Report of the Register of Copyright (1983) suggests that this requirement need not be interpreted broadly:

> Libraries may, because of the nature of their collections, or of the building they occupy, reasonably restrict public access—as, for example, by limiting use of collections to high school students and above, or imposing conditions on their users as a prerequisite to access. No one has suggested that the kinds of commonly-encountered practices libraries apply in order to safeguard their collections, or to give priority to "researchers" as opposed to elementary school browsers, somehow takes these institutions outside S108.[44]

The "available to researchers" requirement is less clear. The provision states that the collection must be:

> available not only to researchers affiliated with the library or archives or with the institution of which it is a part, *but also to other persons doing research in a specialized field* . . . (emphasis added)[45]

This provision of availability to "persons doing research in a specialized field" presents the question of how "available" the collection must be in order for a library or archives to be eligible for Section 108 coverage. Many librarians are of the opinion that, if the collection is made available through some form of interlibrary loan, library network, or consortium, the "availability" criterion is satisfied.[46] While this *may* be true for libraries or archives in non-profit institutions (the Copyright

---

43 17 U.S.C. 108(a)(2).
44 *Report of the Register of Copyrights* (January, 1983), p. 76.
45 17 U.S.C. 108(a)(2)(ii).
46 *Report of the Register of Copyrights* (January, 1983), p. 77.

Office believes otherwise[47]), the same cannot readily be said for libraries or archives in for-profit institutions. The Copyright Office stresses that libraries and archives in for-profit institutions must allow all researchers (even employees of competitors) access to their collections in order to claim the Section 108 exemptions:

> A commercial for-profit entity which desires to avail itself of privileges under [section] 108 must make its collections open to the employees of its competitors. . . . There are no expressed or implicit reservations as to what classes of potential patrons may be forbidden entry to a [section] 108 library. The Copyright Office believes that restrictions based on age or educational status may be made without loss of privileges under [section] 108, but that entrepreneurs, who establish libraries on their premises as integral parts of their profit-seeking operations, must make their collections available to all persons doing research in the fields of their collections if they want to make photocopies under [section] 108.[48]

Taking the Copyright Office's stance into consideration, the conservative approach would be for any library or archives (for-profit or non-profit) which is not "open to the public" to adopt a written "access" policy[49] containing the following elements:

(1) Researchers (including non-employees) must be guaranteed physical access to the library or archives collection upon request.

(2) The institution may deny access to an individual based only on age or educational requirements, which should be clearly specified in the policy.

(3) The institution may place reasonable restrictions on access to the physical collection. For example, the institution may require that a researcher make a formal appointment to use the collection. The institution may also place restrictions on hours of access.

(4) The institution may restrict certain parts of the collection if

---

47 "A library whose collections are available only 'through interlibrary loan of materials' should not fairly be said to have met the standards set out in S108(a)(2)," *Report of the Register of Copyrights* (January, 1983), p. 78.

48 *Report of the Register of Copyrights* (January, 1983), p. 78–79.

49 See Appendix 9 for sample "access" policy.

the majority of the collection is made available. For example, a library or archives may have rare or deteriorating materials which could be damaged if mishandled; such collections could reasonably be kept unavailable. Also, certain proprietory research reports could be restricted.

Notice of Copyright

Section 108(a)(3) provides that "the reproduction or distribution of the work includes a notice of copyright."[50]

Although the statute does not specify language for this "notice," it is likely that most good faith attempts to affix "notice of copyright" to the photocopy will be acceptable. For example, it would be sufficient for a library or archives providing a requested photocopy to include a copy of the title page (or verso) showing the copyright notice. Or, the library or archives may wish to stamp each photocopy with a standard "notice." The American Library Association recommends that the following statement be affixed to the photocopy: "Notice: This material may be protected by copyright law (Title 17 U.S. Code)."[51]

SECTION 108(a) CRITERIA IN RELATION TO FAIR USE OR CONTRACTS

Section 108(f)(4) provides that nothing in Section 108:

> in any way affects the right of fair use as provided by section 107, or any contractual obligations assumed at any time by the library or archives when it obtained a copy or phonorecord of a work in its collections.[52]

Section 108(f)(4) provides that, even though the three criteria listed in Section 108(a) might *not* be met, photocopying a certain item may still be permitted under the fair use provisions of Section 107 or by contract.

Conversely, even if the three criteria *are* met, photocopying a certain item may be prohibited by a contractual arrangement between the

---

50 17 U.S.C. 108(a)(3).
51 Jerome K. Miller, *Applying the new copyright law: a guide for educators & librarians* (Chicago: American Library Assn., 1979), p. 66, *citing* "Warning notices for copies and machines," *American Libraries* 8 (November 1977): 530.
52 17 U.S.C. 108(f)(4).

copyright holder and the library or archives. For example, some city directories are sold with the express restriction that they not be photocopied. Libraries agreeing to the restrictions could not rely on section 108 to allow reproduction of pages from such directories. Other contracts restricting copying privileges are offered by the Copyright Clearance Center (see Chapter Nine).

Fair Use

Section 107 of the Copyright Act of 1976 provides certain exceptions to the copyright holder's exclusive rights enumerated under Section 106. Pursuant to Section 107, photocopies of copyrighted materials may be made for purposes such as "criticism, comment, news reporting, teaching (including multiple copies for classroom use), scholarship, or research,"[53] without infringement of copyright. Section 107 lists four factors to be considered in determining whether a particular use is "fair use":

(1) the purpose and character of the use, including whether such use is of a commercial nature or is for nonprofit educational purposes;

(2) the nature of the copyrighted work;

(3) the amount and substantiality of the portion used in relation to the copyrighted work as a whole; and

(4) the effect of the use upon the potential market for or value of the copyrighted work.[54]

If a photocopying use falls within the four factors of Section 107, it is a "fair use" and is permitted, even though the three criteria listed in Section 108(a) may not be met. Section 108(f)(4) provides that the Section 108 exceptions allowed libraries and archives are in addition to Section 107 exceptions, not further restrictions on "fair use." See Chapter Seven for further discussion of "fair use".

Contractual Arrangements

Similarly, if a library or archives has a contractual arrangement with a copyright holder which allows the library or archives to make or

---

53   17 U.S.C. 107.
54   17 U.S.C. 107.

distribute a copy or multiple copies of a work or part of a work, the restrictions placed on photocopying by Section 108 will not apply. In effect, this type of contractual arrangement is merely a form of the copyright holder granting written permission for use of his or her work.

On the other hand, it is also possible for a library or archives to enter into a contractual arrangement with a copyright holder whereby the library or archives agrees not to copy the work, even though Section 108 would have otherwise permitted the copying. Under section 108(f)(4), a library or archives could not contractually agree not to copy a work and then make copies, claiming an exception under of Section 108. This type of contractual agreement involves, in effect, a waiver of the Section 108 rights of the library or archives.

One example of this type of contractual waiver is a standardized test or answers to a standardized test. Usually when an institution purchases standardized test materials, it agrees not to make or distribute copies of those materials. That agreement not to make copies would prevail over any Section 108 exceptions which might otherwise apply.

Another example of a contractual arrangement which would prevail over Section 108 is the purchase of a play script. Usually, when play scripts are sold, the purchaser is required to buy a specified number of scripts (at a price which includes performance royalties) in order to obtain permission to perform the play. The purchaser agrees not to make and distribute any additional copies of the script. Occasionally, a distributor may enter into an agreement to waive the royalty fees for performance rights and sell a play script to a library or archives. The agreement may state that the play will not be performed publicly, and that the script will be retained by the library or archives for research purposes only. The library or archives may also agree not to make or distribute copies of the play script. If a library or archives enters into such an agreement, that library or archives may not make and distribute photocopies of the play script, even if all requirements of Section 108 are met.

A contract may also grant permission to copy in excess of section 108 or fair use. For example, some types of computer software used by schools and colleges are sold as "lab packs" or "site licenses." These packages include authorization to duplicate the software, in its entirety and in multiple copies.

WORKS NOT COVERED BY SECTION 108

The exceptions to the exclusive rights of reproduction afforded libraries and archives by Section 108 do not include all copyrighted materials in the library's or archives' collection. Section 108(h) specifies that:

> The rights of reproduction and distribution under this section do not apply to a musical work, a pictorial, graphic or sculptural work, or a motion picture or other audiovisual work other than an audiovisual work dealing with news, except that no such limitation shall apply with respect to rights granted by subsections (b) and (c), or with respect to pictorial or graphic works published as illustrations, diagrams, or similar adjuncts to works of which copies are reproduced or distributed in accordance with subsections (d) and (e).[55]

Pursuant to Section 108(h), libraries or archives may not rely on Section 108 exceptions to make and distribute unauthorized photocopies of musical, pictorial, graphic, sculptural, or audiovisual works, unless the photocopying of those works falls within the rights granted by Section 108(b), 108(c), 108(d), or 108(e). For example, library patrons frequently request photocopies of sheet music. Because "musical works" are not covered by section 108 and because this photocopying does not fall under sections 108(b), (c), (d), or (e), the library or archives may only duplicate the sheet music if the music is duplicated for a library's or archives' collection under section 108(b) or (c). Duplication of sheet music for patrons may be permissible "fair use" if only a small portion (for example, one line) is copied.

Copying Complete Published and Unpublished Works

Section 108(b) refers to the right to make and distribute a copy of an unpublished work for purposes of preservation and security. Section 108(c) refers to the right to make a copy of a published work which is damaged, deteriorating, lost, or stolen if an unused, fairly-priced replacement cannot be obtained. See Chapter Four for a more detailed explanation of these subsections.

---

55   17 U.S.C. 108(h).

Copying Artwork in Books and Periodicals

Section 108(h) permits copying pictorial or graphic works published as illustrations, diagrams, etc., if the copies are made and distributed pursuant to Section 108(d) or 108(e). See Chapter Five for a more detailed explanation of these subsections.

SUMMARY

This chapter covers the eligibility of libraries and archives for the section 108 exemption to the exclusive right of reproduction. Section 108(a) of the Copyright Act of 1976 provides that a library or archives is eligible for the duplication exemption if it meets three criteria: no direct or indirect commercial advantage, open to the public, and notice of copyright.

Section 108(f)(4) provides that section 108 does not affect a user's rights under section 107 (fair use). That is, a user in a non-eligible library or archives may still be able to duplicate certain material under section 107. Section 108(f)(4) also provides that section 108 does not affect contractual obligations assumed by the library or archives. That is, a library or archives may not rely on the section 108 exemption if it has entered into a contractual agreement with the copyright holder not to duplicate the material.

In addition to stipulating which types of libraries and archives are eligible for the duplication exemption, section 108 also specifies that certain works are not covered by section 108. Section 108(h) indicates that, with some exceptions, the duplication exemption does not apply to a musical work, a pictorial, graphic or sculptural work, or a motion picture or other audiovisual work other than an audiovisual work dealing with news.

Chapter 4

DUPLICATION FOR LIBRARY USE

This Chapter treats permissible reproduction of materials for inclusion in the library's or archives' collection. Section 108 of the Copyright Act of 1976 allows limited duplication by libraries and archives for their collections (1) if the work is unpublished[56] or (2) if the work is damaged, deteriorating, lost, or stolen.[57]

UNPUBLISHED WORKS

Librarians and archivists may believe that unpublished works, especially older unpublished works, are not protected by copyright. This may not be the case, as shown by section 303 of the Copyright Act of 1976:

> Copyright in a work created before January 1, 1978, but not theretofore in the public domain or copyrighted, subsists from January 1, 1978, and endures for the term provided by section 302. In no case, however, shall the term of copyright in such work expire before December 31, 2002; and, if the work is published on or before December 31, 2002, the term of copyright shall not expire before December 31, 2027.[58]

---

56 17 U.S.C. 108(b).

57 17 U.S.C. 108(c).

58 17 U.S.C. 303. For a detailed discussion of the legislative history and concerns related to copying unpublished personal papers, *see* Linda M. Matthews, "Copyright and the duplication of personal papers in archival repositories," *Library Trends* 32 (Fall, 1983): 223-240.

Although unpublished works may be protected by copyright until December 31, 2002, libraries and archives may still be able to photocopy these unpublished works under section 108(b):

> The rights of reproduction or distribution under this section apply to a copy or phonorecord of an unpublished work duplicated in facsimile form solely for purposes of preservation and security or for deposit for research use in another library or archives of the type described by clause (2) of subsection (a), if the copy or phonorecord reproduced is currently in the collections of the library or archives.[59]

Section 108(b) permits duplication of unpublished works only for purposes of preservation and security. The House Report indicates that this right extends:

> to any type of work, including photographs, motion pictures and sound recordings. Under this exemption, for example, a repository could make photocopies of manuscripts by microfilm or electrostatic process, but could not reproduce the work in "machine-readable" language for storage in an information system.[60]

For example, a library or archives may have a collection of original manuscripts, correspondence, and other papers of interest to scholars. Rather than allowing the researchers to handle the actual documents (which may be fragile or which may become damaged from frequent use), the library or archives may elect to duplicate them for use by researchers. The originals would then be safely preserved in an archival collection for use only by certain personnel.

Copies of unpublished works may be made under section 108(b) only for the library's or archives' own collection or for deposit for research use in another library or archives; section 108(b) does not allow for distribution of copies of unpublished works to library patrons. In other words, although a library or archives may photocopy an entire unpublished work for its own collection or that of another library or archives, it may not photocopy an entire unpublished work for an individual. The House Reports comments on this issue:

---

59   17 U.S.C. 108(b).
60   H.R. Rep. No. 1476, p. 75.

[N]o facsimile copies or phonorecords made under this section can be distributed to scholars or the public; if they leave the institution that reproduced them, they must be deposited for research purposes in another "nonprofit institution" that has archival custody over collections of manuscripts, documents, or other unpublished works of value to scholarly research.[61]

A common practice is to deposit the copy with an institution which then lends the item to the patron on a "long-term loan" basis. This technique is used by historians to obtain extensive files of archival materials or rare books owned by another library or archives. In many instances, the loan is made on an indefinite basis, and the items may remain in the patron's private study until after the scholar is dead.

An individual may not claim that it is "fair use" to photocopy an entire unpublished work for research purposes. This is supported by the Senate Report which provides:

The applicability of the fair use doctrine to unpublished works is narrowly limited since, although the work is unavailable, this is the result of a deliberate choice on the part of the copyright owner. Under ordinary circumstances the copyright owner's "right of first publication" would outweigh any needs or reproduction for classroom purposes.[62]

PUBLISHED WORKS

Section 108(c) permits libraries and archives to copy a published work in its entirety under limited circumstances:

The right of reproduction under this section applies to a copy or phonorecord of a published work duplicated in facsimile form solely for the purpose of replacement of a copy or phonorecord that is damaged, deteriorating, lost, or stolen, if the library or archives has, after a reasonable effort, determined that an unused replacement cannot be obtained at a fair price.[63]

Before duplicating an entire published work under section 108(c), the library or archives must meet two criteria: (1) the library's or

---

61 H.R. Rep. No. 83, 90th Cong., 1st Sess. (1967), p. 38.
62 S. Rep. No. 473, p. 64.
63 17 U.S.C. 108(c).

archives' original copy of the published work must be damaged, deteriorating, lost, or stolen, and (2) the library or archives must have determined, after a reasonable search, that an unused, fairly-priced replacement is unavailable. Both of these criteria must be met for the copying to be permissible under this section.

Damaged, deteriorating, lost, or stolen

Before duplicating an entire published work, the library or archives must be able to show that its original copy was "damaged, deteriorating, lost, or stolen." The key factor here is that the item must *already* be "damaged, deteriorating, lost, or stolen." A library or archives may not make an "archival" copy merely in anticipation that the work will become damaged, deteriorated, lost, or stolen.

This provision may be somewhat frustrating for librarians who feel that it is "unfair" for the library to be required to purchase multiple replacements for certain items which are prone to theft or destruction by library patrons (for example, audiocassettes seem to take more than their fair share of patron abuse). As "unfair" as this criterion may be perceived by librarians, copies may not be made under section 108(c) unless the library's current copy is already "damaged, deteriorating, lost, or stolen" and an unused replacement is unavailable. An answer to this dilemma might be for the library or archives to purchase two copies of items which are likely to become damaged, etc., and to circulate only one of the copies, keeping the second as a non-circulating, archival copy.

Unavailability of unused replacement

Under the second criterion, the library or archives must be able to show that it made a reasonable effort to obtain an unused replacement and that it was unsuccessful in locating one at a fair price. This brings up the questions of (1) "what is a reasonable effort?" and (2) "what is a fair price?" The House Report addressed the first question, stating:

> The scope and nature of a reasonable investigation to determine that an unused replacement cannot be obtained will vary according to the circumstances of a particular situation. It will always require recourse to commonly-known trade sources in the United States, and in the normal situation also to the publisher or other copyright owner (if such owner can

be located at the address listed in the copyright registration), or an authorized reproducing service.[64]

The question of a definition of a "fair price" has been addressed by the Copyright Office in its 1983 report on section 108:

> It seems clear to the Copyright Office that if, for example, a book or periodical is available from its publisher, or from a dealer specializing in "remainders," or from a jobber or dealer in bulk issues of periodicals, the market price will be "fair" and must be met, if copies are available from such sources. If, on the other hand, the only unused copies are available at high prices from merchants specializing in rare or antique books, then copying may be authorized. A note of caution should be sounded, however: a high price is not definitionally unfair. Certain works, particularly those dealing with time-sensitive financial information, are available only at a price which one might fairly call "high." Should a copy of such a work be lost or stolen, it would have to be replaced by meeting the publisher's price as long as unused replacement copies were available.[65]

The American Library Association has also addressed the question of "fair price," stating that it should be "as close as possible to the latest suggested retail price."[66]

MUSICAL, PICTORIAL, GRAPHIC, AND AUDIOVISUAL WORKS

Section 108(h) provides:

> The rights of reproduction and distribution under this section do not apply to a musical work, a pictorial, graphic or sculptural work, or a motion picture or other audiovisual work other than an audiovisual work dealing with news, *except that no such limitation shall apply with respect to rights granted by subsections (b) and (c).* [Emphasis supplied.][67]

---

64 H.R. Rep. No. 1476, p. 75–76.

65 *Report of the Register of Copyrights* (January, 1983), p. 107–108.

66 Jerome K. Miller, *Applying the new copyright law: a guide for educators and librarians* (Chicago: ALA, 1979), p. 73 *citing* ALA, Resources and Technical Services Division, Implementation of the Copyright Revision Act Committee, "Guidelines for seeking or making a copy of an entire copyrighted work for a library, archives or user" (Chicago: The Committee, no date), unpaged.

67 17 U.S.C. 108(h).

Read together with sections 108(b) and (c), section 108(h) permits duplication of entire unpublished or published works of many types, including (but not limited to) "a musical work, a pictorial, graphic or sculptural work, or a motion picture or other audiovisual work. "[68] With some exceptions, duplication of these specific works is not permitted under the other provisions of section 108, in particular, photocopying for individual library patrons. See Chapter Five for detailed coverage of this issue.

AUDIOVISUAL NEWS PROGRAMS

In addition to the duplication rights granted by sections 108(b) and (c), libraries and archives are also permitted to make and distribute copies of audiovisual news programs. Section 108(f)(3) states that nothing in section 108:

> shall be construed to limit the reproduction and distribution by lending of a limited number of copies and excerpts by a library or archives of an audiovisual news program, subject to clauses (1), (2), and (3) of subsection (a)[69]

This "audiovisual news program" provision was added to protect Vanderbilt University's archival collection of news videotapes. The Senate Report explained the exemption as follows:

> The purpose of this clause is to prevent the copyright law from precluding such operations as the Vanderbilt University Television News Archive, which makes videotape recordings of television news programs, prepares indexes of the contents, and leases copies of complete broadcasts or compilations of coverage of specified subjects for limited periods upon request from scholars and researchers.[70]

The House Report further interpreted the "audiovisual news program" exemption:

> This exemption is intended to apply to the daily newscasts of the national television networks, which report the major events of the day. It does not apply to documentary (except

---

68   17 U.S.C. 108(h).
69   17 U.S.C. 108(f)(3).
70   S. Rep. No. 473, p. 69.

documentary programs involving news reporting as that term is used in section 107), magazine-format or other public affairs broadcasts dealing with subjects of general interest to the viewing public.. . .

[This clause] is intended to permit libraries and archives, subject to the general conditions of this section, to make off-the-air videotape recordings of daily network newscasts for limited distribution to scholars and researchers for use in research purposes. As such, it is an adjunct to the American Television and Radio Archive established in Section 113 of the Act which will be the principal repository for television broadcast material, including news broadcasts.[71]

Because the above statement from the House Report left some doubt as to the Vanderbilt program in relation to the provision, the Conference Report included the following clarification:

The conference committee is aware that an issue has arisen as to the meaning of the phrase "audiovisual news program" in section 108(f)(3).

The conferees believe that, under the provision as adopted in the conference substitute, a library or archives qualifying under section 108(a) would be free, without any regard to the archival activities of the Library of Congress or any other organization, to reproduce, on videotape or any other medium of fixation or reproduction, local, regional, or network newscasts, interviews concerning current news events, and on-the-spot coverage of news events, and to distribute a limited number of reproductions of such a program on a loan basis.[72]

Copies of programs made under this provision are intended only for research and cannot be used in classrooms or reproduced for commercial distribution.

PHOTOCOPYING FOR LIBRARY VERTICAL FILES

Most library holdings include a vertical file collection containing pamphlets, newspaper clippings, and other items of current interest. The question often arises as to whether photocopies of periodical articles or

---

71 H.R. Rep. No. 1476, p. 77.
72 H.R. Rep. No. 1733, p. 73.

chapters from books may be included in the vertical file collection. Under section 108, the answer is simply "no" unless the library or archives has received written permission from the copyright holder.

Photocopying articles or chapters for the vertical file does not fall under any of the permissible uses under section 108 unless the duplication is for replacement of a "damaged, deteriorating, lost, or stolen" item under section 108(c). The library may not rely on sections 108(d) and (e) for vertical file duplication, because those subsections relate only to copies made for *individual* users and must be retained only by that user for personal use. See Chapter Five for a more detailed discussion of sections 108(d) and (e).

Some libraries incorrectly claim "fair use" when they retain photocopies of articles which their patrons have received through interlibrary loan. If a library uses interlibrary loan to obtain photocopies of articles for its vertical file rather than purchasing either the periodical issue or single article reprints from the publisher, the publisher's "potential market" for sale of the issues or reprints has been adversely affected and the fourth criterion of "fair use" has not been met. Section 107 provides:

> In determining whether the use made of a work in any particular case is a fair use the factors to be considered shall include
>
> . . . (4) the effect of the use upon the potential market for or value of the copyrighted work.[73]

Some libraries maintain vertical files on "hot" issues which are requested frequently, such as abortion, drug abuse, recycling, and others. Libraries may not rely on section 108 if they photocopy feature articles on these topics for inclusion in their vertical files, even if they own the original periodical. The vertical file may contain clipped articles from newspapers or periodicals, original pamphlets, and library-prepared bibliographies of current materials, but section 108 does not permit a library to make photocopies and retain them in the vertical file without permission. Most newspaper publishers are generous in granting the permission to duplicate articles from their papers for educational purposes.

---

73   17 U.S.C. 107. See also Chapter 7.

There is an argument that, although photocopying for the vertical file is not permitted under section 108, it may be permissible "fair use" under section 107. This would be true only if the four criteria of "fair use" were met. See Chapter Seven for an explanation of "fair use" and its criteria.

PHOTOCOPYING FOR LIBRARY RESERVE

School and academic libraries are frequently called upon to provide "reserve" copies of articles, chapters, and other materials for student use. See Chapter Six for a detailed discussion of duplication for reserve collections.

SUMMARY

Libraries and archives may make copies of unpublished works solely for purposes of preservation or security. They may duplicate published works only to replace a damaged, deteriorating, lost, or stolen copy if an unused, fairly-priced replacement is unavailable. Duplication permitted in these instances extends to musical, pictorial, graphic, and sculptural works and to motion pictures and other audiovisual works. Audiovisual news programs may be duplicated for library or archival collections such as the Vanderbilt University Television News Archive. A library or archives vertical file may not contain photocopies of copyrighted materials unless written permission has been granted by the copyright owner.

Chapter 5

DUPLICATION FOR PATRON USE

The first part of this chapter examines *supervised* copying of library materials for patrons as defined by sections 108(d) and 108(e). [Limitations in section 108(g) and the National Commission on New Technological Uses of Copyrighted Works (CONTU) guidelines are covered in Chapter Six.] The second part of this chapter covers *unsupervised* copying equipment in a library or archives.

SUPERVISED COPIERS

Section 108 of the Copyright Act of 1976 allows a library or archives to make a single copy of an item for a patron if (1) the amount copied does not exceed the allowable limits set forth in 108(d) (copying a small portion of a work), 108(e) (copying a substantial portion or an entire work), or 108(g) (prohibition against systematic copying), (2) the copy becomes the property of the patron for private study, scholarship, or research, and (3) the library or archives displays a "warning of copyright" at the place where the copies are made.[74]

A library or archives may receive a request for copies under section 108 in one of two ways: (1) a request from a patron or (2) a request

---

74   17 U.S.C. 108(d)–108(g).

for a patron from another library or archives through interlibrary loan.[75] The library or archives may supply copies within the permissible bounds set forth in section 108(d), (e), and (g). Section 108(d) provides for the copying of a small portion of a copyrighted work, as follows:

> The rights of reproduction and distribution under this section apply to a copy, made from the collection of a library or archives where the user makes his or her request or from that of another library or archives, of no more than one article or other contribution to a copyrighted collection or periodical issue, or to a copy or phonorecord of a small part of any other copyrighted work, if—
>
> (1) the copy or phonorecord becomes the property of the user, and the library or archives has had no notice that the copy or phonorecord would be used for any purpose other than private study, scholarship, or research; and
>
> (2) the library or archives displays prominently, at the place where orders are accepted, and includes on its order form, a warning of copyright in accordance with requirements that the Register of Copyrights shall prescribe by regulation.[76]

Section 108(d) enumerates five requirements for making single copies for patrons:

(1) the user must initiate the request;

(2) the copy must be no more than one article or other contribution to a copyrighted collection or periodical issue or a small part of any other work;

(3) the copy must become the property of the user;

(4) the library must have no notice that the copy will be used for any purpose other than private study, scholarship, or research; and

---

75 Note that the term "interlibrary loan" is somewhat of a misnomer in the context of section 108, as the requested photocopies are not on "loan" but rather become the property of the requestor. Before photocopies were readily available, libraries routinely lent the bound volumes of periodicals. The photocopies distributed today are a substitute for the loan of the original.

76 17 U.S.C. 108(d).

(5) the library or archives must display a "warning of copyright" where the orders are accepted and on its order form.

These five requirements are considered separately.

User-Initiated Request

The individual patron must initiate the request for the copy; the library or archives may not initiate the request. Some libraries and archives issue newsletters listing recent books and articles on certain topics, together with the suggestion that patrons come to the library or archives to read or check out the items. It is not permissible for the newsletter article to state that the library or archives will copy the listed articles for patrons. This offer could be construed as "library-initiated" copying which would not fall within the acceptable limits of section 108(d).

No More Than One Article or Other Contribution

Section 108(d) states that the library or archives may make a copy for an individual patron of "no more than one article or other contribution to a copyrighted collection or periodical issue, or to a copy or phonorecord of a small part of any other copyrighted work."[77]

The first part of this "amount" requirement seems clear. If the work is a collection or a periodical issue, copying is limited to a single article or other contribution. This requirement has caused some consternation to librarians as frequently a periodical issue or a collection will contain more than one item on the same topic, several of which may be of interest to an individual patron. This is a significant problem when a patron requests copies of two or three short articles from a periodical such as *Time* or *Newsweek*. The Register of Copyrights has addressed this question in light of the "fair use" provisions of section 107:

> [This] is one area where [section] 107 may have a significant role to play when [section] 108 privileges have been exhausted. Thus, when a patron desires two articles from one issue of a periodical, the "nature of the work" consideration under fair use [17 U.S.C. 107(2)] may include the recognition that the copying of one additional (i.e., "post-108") article from

---

77   17 U.S.C. 108(d).

the proceedings or symposium may be fair use. The copying of another additional "post-108" article should be guarded against.[78]

Although the above statement offers a convincing argument that a second article or contribution may be made under "fair use," it is not clear whether that second copy may be made by the library/archives or by the patron. It is clear, however, that the copying of more than one or two articles or contributions may only be done within the limits set forth in section 108(e).

Under this "amount" requirement, if the work is not a collection or a periodical issue, the library or archives may only copy "a small part" for a patron. There is no clear definition of "a small part," as pointed out by the Register of Copyrights:

> [A] "small part" is, obviously, smaller than the "substantial part" of a work (whose copying is governed by the more stringent regime set out in subsection (e)), but where the boundary lies between them is a proper subject for case-by-case analysis, or, ideally, for agreement among the parties, as in the voluntary guidelines already agreed upon for certain inter-library transactions, off-air taping, and the copying of music.[79]

Although the fair-use guidelines for copying from books and periodicals for classroom distribution apply to section 107 use and not to section 108 use, the guidelines' test for "brevity" could be helpful in determining the definition of a "small part."

The "brevity" test for section 107 provides:

   (i) Poetry: (a) A complete poem if less than 250 words and if printed on not more than two pages or, (b) from a longer poem, an excerpt of not more than 250 words.

   (ii) Prose: (a) Either a complete article, story or essay of less than 2,500 words, or (b) an excerpt from any prose work of not more than 1,000 words or 10% of the work,

---

78 *Report of the Register of Copyrights* (January, 1983), p. 118.

79 *Report of the Register of Copyrights* (January, 1983), p. 117-118.

whichever is less, but in any event a minimum of 500 words.[80]

(iii)Illustration: One chart, graph, diagram, drawing, cartoon or picture per book or per periodical issue.

(iv)"Special" works: Certain works in poetry, prose or in "poetic prose" which often combine language with illustrations and which are intended sometimes for children and at other times for a more general audience fall short of 2,500 words in their entirety. Paragraph "ii" above notwithstanding such "special works" may not be reproduced in their entirety; however, an excerpt comprising not more than two of the published pages of such special work and containing not more than 10% of the words found in the text thereof, may be reproduced.[81]

The term "special works," mentioned above, usually applies to comic books and children's illustrated books.

When considering the "amount" requirement, one also must look at the type of material being copied. Section 108(h) indicates that the reproduction and distribution rights of section 108 do not apply to musical, pictorial, graphic, or sculptural works, or to motion pictures or other audiovisual works, *except* "with respect to pictorial or graphic works published as illustrations, diagrams, or similar adjuncts to works"[82] copied pursuant to sections 108(d) or 108(e). For example, it would not be an infringement to copy several illustrations if they were all included as part of a single article or chapter.

Property of the User

A copy made under section 108(d) must become the property of the user. In other words, neither a library providing a copy nor an intermediary "interlibrary loan" library may require the user to return the copy for inclusion in the library's collection. If, for example, a library

---

80 Each of the numerical limits stated in "i" and "ii" above may be expanded to permit the completion of an unfinished line of a poem or of an unfinished prose paragraph.

81 "Agreement on guidelines for classroom copying in not-for-profit educational institutions," H.R. Rep. No. 1476, Section 107, in *The official fair-use guidelines: complete texts of four official documents arranged for use by educators*, 4th ed. (Friday Harbor, WA: Copyright Information Services, 1989), p. 6-7.

82 17 U.S.C. 108(h).

or archives wishes to add a photocopy of an "interlibrary-loaned" article to its vertical file holdings, the library or archives must obtain written permission from the copyright owner (see Chapter Four regarding vertical file collections and Chapter Nine regarding writing for permission).

Information Brokers

The "property of the user" requirement raises the question of the "information broker" or "free-lance librarian" who procures information from libraries, archives, and other sources for clients for a fee. Such brokers request copies of library materials and then give these copies to a client as part of a research project. Is the library supplying the copies within the bounds of section 108(d) or is this an infringement of copyright? The brokers could claim that this use is not contrary to section 108(d), because they are selling not the *photocopies*, but their *services* to locate the articles. As one broker stated, "What we do has less to do with selling merchandise and more to do with selling a professional service."[83]

On the other hand, the Register of Copyrights states that copies obtained by such brokers are sold for a profit to the clients and thus do not fall within the bounds of permissible copying set forth in section 108(d).[84] The position of the Register of Copyrights is convincing because the copies requested by brokers do not become the property of the actual requestor and because the brokers pass on the cost of the copies to the client, along with other charges. Also, brokers have the options of (1) providing their clients with bibliographies of materials, from which the clients could select relevant articles and personally request them from a library or archives, or (2) obtaining permission to copy the articles for the clients, either through a copyright clearinghouse or direct written permission from the copyright owner.

Although the Register of Copyrights has made his position clear regarding the non-applicability of section 108 to brokers, it is not clear whether this position would extend to all "intermediaries" making photocopies for others. For example, if a professor sends a research assistant to the library to research a question and to photocopy relevant articles

---

83 Kelly Warnken & Barbara Felicetti, eds., *So you want to be an information broker?* (Chicago: Information Alternative, 1982), p. 5.
84 *Report of the Register of Copyrights* (January, 1983), p. 120.

for the professor's research, it is reasonable to assume that such photo-copying would be permitted by section 108. Although the assistant is paid for time spent on research, it is likely that a court would see the assistant and professor as a "research team" and not as part of a client/broker relationship. A research assistantship is more than just a salaried position; it is also intended as a learning activity for a graduate student. The distinction between the broker's relationship with clients and the assistant/professor relationship, or other intermediary relationship, is illustrated by one broker's suggestions regarding billing:

> When computing a bill for services rendered to a client there often are out-of-pocket expenses incurred on behalf of the client that need reimbursement as well. When figuring a client's bill several brokers caution to be sure to include all costs that are not a normal part of your overhead . . .
>
> In many cases . . ., it is appropriate to add a mark up, or service charge, to compensate you for the temporary use of your money on the client's behalf.[85]

Another broker makes it clear that the provision of photocopies is a standard service:

> If the broker provides bibliographies, it should follow that the broker will back that up with document delivery. By document delivery we're not just talking about journal articles. We're talking about annual reports, conference proceedings, environmental impact statements, patents, newspaper articles, descriptions of research in progress, directories, dissertations, congressional hearings, state and federal legislation, industry standards and so on.[86]

Notice of Use Other Than Private Study, Scholarship, or Research

Section 108(d) provides that the library or archives supplying the copy must have "no notice that the copy or phonorecord would be used for any purpose other than private study, scholarship, or research."[87]

---

85   Alice Sizer Warner, *Mind your own business* (Chicago: Neal-Schuman Pubs., 1987), p. 65.
86   Warnken, p. 8.
87   17 U.S.C. 108(d)(1).

As with the requirement of "property of the user," this "private study" requirement raises the question of copying for brokers. The Register of Copyrights states:

> If a person seeking a photocopy (whether locally or via ILL) works for *any* information broker, then the purpose of the copying is *not* "private study, scholarship, or research." *If* the library has notice of such person's status, then [section] 108 does not authorize the copying.[88]

The provision states that the library or archives must have "no notice" of an unauthorized purpose for copying the material. Although the term "notice" is not defined in the Copyright Act of 1976, it is defined elsewhere in law. The Register of Copyrights refers to the definition provided by the Uniform Commercial Code, which states:

> A person has "notice" of a fact when
>
> (a) he has actual knowledge of it; or
>
> (b) he has received a notice or notification of it; or
>
> (c) from all the facts and circumstances known to him at the time in question he has reason to know that it exists.[89]

With this definition for a guideline, a library or archives would have notice of the "purpose other than private study, scholarship, or research" (1) if the staff had been directly told of the purpose (either by the requester or by a third party) or (2) if the staff had reason to know based on obvious facts. The meaning of "notice" is easily shown through examples.

In the first situation, it is not uncommon for patrons to chat with library staff regarding the items they are having photocopied. For example, a patron may reveal that he or she is an "information broker" and is having the copies made for a client. Or, the patron may reveal that he or she plans to include the copy in a commercial publication. Or, a third party may point out to the staff, either in person or by written communication, that a certain patron is a broker and is selling the copies

---

88 *Report of the Register of Copyrights* (January, 1983), p. 120.
89 *Report of the Register of Copyrights* (January, 1983), p. 120, *citing* American Law Institute, Uniform Commercial Code Sec. 1–201(25) (1978).

procured at the library. In these examples, the library or archives has direct knowledge, or "notice," that the copies will not be used for private study, scholarship, or research.

In the second situation, circumstances in a particular case may give the library or archives "notice," even though no one may have directly informed the library staff of the actual use of the copies. For example, the library would be "on notice" or have "reason to know" if a particular patron (who frequently requested articles on ILL) put an advertisement in a local paper offering his or her services as an "information broker" or "free-lance" librarian.

Some academic libraries provide locked carrels or small office space to commercial information brokers, who in turn provide specialized services for local businesses and others. These information brokers may or may not be able to provide photocopies under section 108, depending on the extent to which the service is tied into the library's program and whether the library or the local business compensates the broker for services.

Warning of Copyright

Section 108(d)(2) requires the library or archives to display prominently where copying orders are accepted, and to include on the order form, "a warning of copyright in accordance with requirements that the Register of Copyrights shall prescribe by regulation."[90] The Register specified the following notice:

NOTICE
Warning Concerning Copyright Restrictions

The copyright law of the United States (Title 17, United States Code) governs the making of photocopies or other reproductions of copyrighted materials.

Under certain conditions specified by law, libraries and archives are authorized to furnish a photocopy or other reproduction. One of these specified conditions is that the photocopy or reproduction is not to be 'used for any purpose other than private study, scholarship, or research.' If a user makes a re-

---

90   17 U.S.C. 108(d)(2).

quest for, or later uses, a photocopy or reproduction for purposes in excess of 'fair use,' that user may be liable for copyright infringement.

This institution reserves the right to refuse to accept a
copying order, if in its judgment, fulfillment of the order would
involve violation of copyright law.[91]

This "Warning of Copyright" must be prominently displayed
where orders are taken for photocopies. The regulation states that the
"Warning" must be printed in eighteen-point type or larger on heavy
paper or other durable material.[92]

The "Warning" must also be included on order forms for photocopies and for patron interlibrary loan request forms (although it is not
necessary to include the "Warning" on ILL forms sent between libraries). The type size must be no smaller that eight-point and must be
"clearly legible, comprehensible, and readily apparent to a casual reader
of the form."[93] The question has arisen regarding libraries or archives
which do not have written forms for patron requests for photocopying
or for ILL. This question has been addressed by Dr. Miller:

Some libraries do not ask patrons to submit a written
request for staff copying or for interlibrary loans. The writer
believes that these libraries need not introduce copying request
forms merely to comply with this part of the regulation. The
notice must only appear on request forms, where such forms
are used.[94]

COPYING ENTIRE WORKS FOR PATRONS

Section 108(e) allows copying of entire works, or substantial parts
of works, in a library's or archives' collection: (1) if the copy becomes
the property of the user, (2) if the library or archives has no notice that
the copy will be used for any purpose other than private study, scholarship, or research, (3) if the library or archives displays the proper
"Warning of copyright", and (4) if "the library or archives has first determined, on the basis of a reasonable investigation, that a copy or

---

91   37 C.F.R. 201.14.
92   37 C.F.R. 201.14.
93   37 C.F.R. 201.14.
94   Miller, *Applying the new copyright law*, p. 68.

phonorecord of the copyrighted work cannot be obtained at a pair [sic] price."[95]

The first three requirements listed above have been discussed in detail earlier in this chapter and do not need to be repeated here. The fourth requirement, however, deserves a close examination as it is the only requirement which differentiates between copying a "small part of a work" (section 108(d)) and copying "substantial parts" or "entire" works. Before a library or archives may copy a substantial part of a work, or an entire work, for a patron, the library or archives must first determine that a "reasonable investigation" has been conducted and that an "original" copy cannot be found at a fair price. The reasonable search for a copy of an out-of-print book should include a search for microfiche copies, as well as for bound copies.

This requirement brings up two questions addressed in Chapter Four in the context of section 108(c): (1) what is a "reasonable investigation"? and (2) what is a "fair price"? The only difference under section 108(e) appears to be that "a library must seek to buy used as well as unused copies of the work at a fair price, and fail to find any available."[96]

This requirement also brings rise to the question of what is meant by "substantial parts" of a work. The Register of Copyrights addressed this question, stating:

> The difference is that "(e)" transactions involve the photocopying of entire works or substantial parts thereof. Again, the boundary between the "small part" governed by (d) and the "substantial part" covered by (e) is not a bright line clearly drawn in the statute. It is, rather, best left to resolution by the parties or, should that prove impossible, by the courts.[97]

Some university and large public libraries offer microfilm reproduction services for out-of-print books. Libraries and archives which provide microfilm services must follow the requirements of section 108 when duplicating out-of-print materials, no matter what format is used

---

95 17 U.S.C. 108(e).
96 *Report of the Register of Copyrights* (January, 1983), p. 123.
97 *Report of the Register of Copyrights* (January, 1983), p. 122.

for duplication. Section 108 applies to microform copies, as well as to photocopying and other methods of duplication.

UNSUPERVISED COPIERS

In limited circumstances, a library or archives will not be liable as a "co-infringer" for a patron's unauthorized copying. Section 108(f)(1) provides that nothing in section 108:

> shall be construed to impose liability for copyright infringement upon a library or archives or its employees for the unsupervised use of reproducing equipment located on its premises: *Provided*, That such equipment displays a notice that the making of a copy may be subject to the copyright law.[98]

The patron who makes the "infringing" copies, however, is not protected by section 108(f)(1), as indicated in section 108(f)(2):

> Nothing in this section—
>
> (2) excuses a person who uses such reproducing equipment or who requests a copy or phonorecord under subsection (d) from liability for copyright infringement for any such act, or for any later use of such copy or phonorecord, if it exceeds fair use as provided by section 107.[99]

A library or archives will not be liable for copyright infringement under the provisions of section 108(f)(1) if two criteria are met: (1) the copying done on the library's or archives' duplicating equipment is "unsupervised" and (2) a copyright warning notice is displayed near the unsupervised equipment.

The first criterion requires "unsupervised use" of the reproducing equipment located on the library's or archives' premises. Although the statute does not define "unsupervised," common sense should aid a library or archives in identifying which copiers are "supervised" and which are "unsupervised." Obviously, a library staff member making copies for a patron constitutes "supervised" use. The Register of Copyrights suggests that in the case of a corporation library, copying by cor-

---

98 17 U.S.C. 108(f)(1).
99 17 U.S.C. 108(f)(2).

porate employees (whether library employees or not) constitutes "supervised" copying.[100]

On the other hand, coin-operated copiers which are provided for patron use and for which staff assistance is not offered would constitute "unsupervised" within section 108(f)(1). Likewise, it could be argued that key-operated or auditron-operated copiers upon which patrons do their own copying are also "unsupervised." In those situations, the patrons make their own copies and then pay library staff members based on the number of copies made.

The question of "supervised" versus "unsupervised" is not clear-cut. Some authorities have suggested that even coin-operated or other patron-operated copiers may actually be "supervised" based on their proximity to library staff work stations. Dr. Miller states:

> It may be safe to assume that a self-service copier located near and in sight of a staff work station is not truly an unsupervised machine.
>
> One should not assume from this that all self-service copying machines must be located in an obscure corner, but some prudence should be exercised in placing these machines far enough from a staff work station that the staff cannot readily see what is being copied. Some smaller libraries use an honor system to collect copying fees from self-service copiers. . . . In some situations, this may fall with [the] definition of supervision.[101]

The second criterion requires a warning notice to be displayed on the unsupervised equipment stating that the making of a copy may be subject to the copyright law. The Register of Copyrights has not prescribed specific language for this notice, but the American Library Association recommends the following:

> Notice: The copyright law of the United States (Title 17 U.S. Code) governs the making of photocopies or other repro-

---

100 *Report of the Register of Copyrights* (January, 1983), p. 145-147.
101 Miller, *Applying the new copyright law*, p. 71.

ductions of copyrighted material. The person using this equipment is liable for any infringement.[102]

Placement of this notice, or similar language, should be sufficient to satisfy the "warning notice" criterion for unsupervised copiers. This notice should be placed on all types of duplication equipment, including microfiche reader-printers.

SUMMARY

Libraries and archives may make singles copies of small parts of copyrighted library materials for a patron's use if the copies (1) are supplied at the patron's request, (2) become the property of the patron, and (3) are used for private study, scholarship, or research. The library or archives must prominently display a "Warning of Copyright" where requests for copies are taken. Libraries and archives may also copy substantial parts of works, or even entire works, for patrons if the above requirements are met, *and* if a reasonable investigation has failed to produce a fairly-priced copy of the work.

If a library or archives makes available "unsupervised" copiers for patron use, the library or archives will not be liable for copyright infringement if a notice is displayed which states that the making of a copy may be subject to the copyright law.

---

102 "Three words added to copyright notice," *American Libraries* 9 (January, 1978): p. 22.

Chapter 6

SYSTEMATIC REPRODUCTION AND OTHER MULTIPLE-COPY ISSUES

The first part of this chapter covers "systematic reproduction" of copyrighted materials which is prohibited by section 108(g) of the Copyright Act. The second part examines the CONTU guidelines for duplicating articles for interlibrary loan. The final part considers duplicating materials for "reserve" collections and other multiple-copy duplication which may be permitted under the "fair use" provisions of section 107.

SYSTEMATIC REPRODUCTION

Section 108(g) prohibits systematic reproduction as follows:

> The rights of reproduction and distribution under this section extend to the isolated and unrelated reproduction or distribution of a single copy or phonorecord of the same material on separate occasions, but do not extend to cases where the library or archives, or its employee—
>
> (1) is aware or has substantial reason to believe that it is engaging in the related or concerted reproduction or distribution of multiple copies or phonorecords of the same material, whether made on one occasion or over a period of time, and whether intended for aggregate use by one or more individual members of a group; or
>
> (2) engages in the systematic reproduction or distribution of single or multiple copies or phonorecords of material

> described in subsection (d): *Provided,* That nothing in this clause prevents a library or archives from participating in interlibrary arrangements that do not have, as their purpose or effect, that the library or archives receiving such copies or phonorecords for distribution does so in such aggregate quantities as to substitute for a subscription to or purchase of such work.[103]

The section 108(g) prohibition on systematic reproduction includes any photocopying done on a "standing order" basis for patrons, the library itself, or other libraries or archives. To reproduce and distribute copies on a systematic basis, the library or archives must obtain written permission from the copyright holder.

For example, several periodicals have regular columns which appear in every issue. If a professor asks an academic library to watch for the monthly issues of a certain periodical and to photocopy and deliver a specific column automatically (without the professor's having to ask each month), this appears to be systematic copying. This "standing order" photocopying request would be considered "systematic reproduction [and] distribution of single . . . copies"[104] which is prohibited by section 108(g)(2).

The U.S. Copyright Office defines "systematic" copying:

> if a corporate library's action, in photocopying periodical articles or short portions of other works, is done in accordance with a general plan, system, or routine, then it must be authorized by the copyright owner. For example, any firm whose library, as a regular practice, prepares photocopies of recently received journal articles for circulation in the firm, should obtain copyright permission to do so, since such a practice is systematic.[105]

Another example of prohibited systematic reproduction and distribution is the common practice of photocopying and circulating the table of contents pages of current periodicals as they are received by

---

103 17 U.S.C. 108(g).

104 17 U.S.C. 108(g)(2).

105 *Report of the Register of Copyrights* (January, 1983), p. 85. The Copyright Clearance Center has been pressuring corporate libraries to contract for copying rights to cover this situation.

the library. This is frequently done in medical, academic, and other special libraries where patrons need to be updated quickly on current developments in their fields. Although some scholarly periodicals state that they permit duplication of the table of contents, most do not. In cases where the table of contents is protected by copyright, the library or archives using this current awareness service must first obtain written permission from the copyright holder.

Permission is requested to copy the table of contents pages from all future issues, so that only one request/permission letter is necessary. An alternative, which some libraries still employ, is to circulate the actual periodicals to the users. Although this alternative avoids systematic reproduction of the table of contents pages, several libraries have found it unattractive because the circulated periodicals are often "lost" in the process or take several months to return to the library, thus making them unavailable to other library users.

The practice of photocopying the table of contents (even with written permission) brings up another interesting copyright infringement question. If the library circulates the table of contents with the suggestion that the users come to the library to read the articles, there is probably no infringement on the part of the library, even if the users come to the library and make copies on unsupervised equipment in excess of amounts permitted by section 108.[106] If, on the other hand, the library circulates the table of contents with the suggestion that the user contact the library to receive photocopies of desired articles, the photocopying does not comply with the section 108 exemption. Section 108(d) indicates that the section 108 exception applies to situations where the *user* requests the copy.[107] The exception does not appear to apply to situations where the library or archives initiates the request for photocopying.[108]

THE CONTU GUIDELINES AND INTERLIBRARY LOAN POLICIES

Section 108(g)(2) provides that libraries or archives may participate

---

106 Although see Chapter 5 regarding the library's liability for knowledge of unauthorized copies made by users on unsupervised equipment.
107 17 U.S.C. 108(d).
108 See Chapter 5 for more complete coverage of user-initiated requests.

in interlibrary arrangements that do not have, as their purpose or effect, that the library or archives receiving such copies
or phonorecords for distribution does so in such aggregate quantities as to substitute for a subscription to or purchase of such
a work.[109]

The National Commission on New Technological Uses of Copyrighted Works (CONTU) consulted with library, publisher, and author
organizations to define the "aggregate quantities" of section 108(g)(2)
and developed a set of guidelines.[110] CONTU presented the set of guidelines to the House and Senate subcommittees as a workable interpretation of section 108(g)(2) in relation to interlibrary loan photocopying
of periodical articles published within five years of the date of the interlibrary loan request.

The basic components of the CONTU guidelines are as follows:

1. The guidelines only apply to periodical issues published
    within five years of the user's request.

2. Within one calendar year, a requesting library or archives may
    receive no more than five copies of an article or articles pub-
    lished in any given periodical. This includes all issues of the
    periodical published in the last five years, as opposed to a
    single issue of the periodical.

3. Interlibrary loan requests for copies or phonorecords of other
    materials, such as fiction, poetry, contributions to copy-
    righted collections, or a small part of any other copyrighted
    work,[111] may not exceed five copies or phonorecords "of or
    from any given work (including a collective work) during the
    entire period when such material shall be protected by copy-
    right."[112]

4. If the library or archives which is requesting the article has
    subscribed to a periodical or has ordered other copyrighted
    materials, but they are not available, the duplication will not

---

109 17 U.S.C. 108(g)(2).
110 See Appendix 8 for complete text of the CONTU Guidelines (H.R. Rep. No. 1733).
111 17 U.S.C. 108(d).
112 H.R. Rep. No. 1733, p. 73.

be considered as "interlibrary loan." Rather, requirements for such duplication will fall under section 108 provisions for copying from the library's or archives' own collections.

5. Requests for copies or phonorecords of materials may not be filled unless the library or archives states that the request conforms to the CONTU guidelines.

6. The requesting library or archives must maintain records of all duplication requests it makes and retain the records for three years after the end of the year in which the request was made.

7. The CONTU guidelines shall be reviewed not later than five years from the date of the Copyright Act, as part of the review required by section 108(i).[113]

Although the CONTU guidelines have helped to facilitate interlibrary loan transactions, they also created controversy in two areas: (1) interpretation of the five-year rule and (2) the requesting library's representation of compliance.

Interpretation of the Five-Year Rule

Because the CONTU guidelines are limited to materials which are less than five years old, the guidelines have been inaccurately "construed to mean that the duration of copyright is *five* years, rather than 75 years or 50 years after the death of the author as provided in the law."[114] Some librarians have mistakenly assumed that the CONTU guidelines permit unlimited copying from materials five or more years old. The Register of Copyrights states:

> the five-year portion of the CONTU guidelines, although felt by many to be appropriate, may have had the effect of creating the false impression that the term of copyright is no more than the scope of the guidelines.[115]

---

113 The first five-year review under section 108(i) was reported in *Report of the Register of Copyrights: library reproduction of copyrighted works* (17 U.S.C. 108) (Washington, DC: January, 1983); the second five-year review was reported by the Register of Copyrights in January 1988.

114 *Report of the Register of Copyrights* (January, 1983), p. 134.

115 *Report of the Register of Copyrights* (January, 1983), p. 135.

On the contrary, duplication of copyrighted materials which are five or more years old must meet section 108 or section 107 criteria for reproduction. The CONTU guidelines were not intended to terminate the copyright holder's exclusive right to reproduction after only five years.

The Requesting Library's Representation of Compliance

The CONTU guidelines state that:

> No request for a copy or phonorecord of any material to which these guidelines apply may be fulfilled by the supplying entity unless such request is accompanied by a representation by the requesting entity that the request was made in conformity with these guidelines.[116]

In 1977 the American Library Association (ALA) developed an interlibrary loan form to comply with this guideline which includes the following provision:

Request complies with

☐ 108(g)(2) Guidelines (CCG)

☐ other provisions of copyright law (CCL).[117]

The ALA interlibrary loan form indicates that the first box is to be checked for transactions which comply with the CONTU guidelines' requirements. The second box is to be checked if the transaction "is sanctioned under parts of the law other than Subsection 108(d) as qualified by 108(g)(2)" and the CONTU guidelines.[118] The Register of Copyrights asserts that the form's options are too limited and suggests that

> the full regime inherent in [sections] 106–108 of the copyright law should be manifest on the form. That is, consideration of the total proscription on systematic copying *except* in certain ILL transactions and of the general proscription on related or concerted copying could be stated in conjunction with

---

116 H.R. Rep. No. 1733, p. 73.
117 "Copyright law prompts new ILL form," *American Libraries* 18 (October, 1977): 492-B.
118 "Copyright law prompts new ILL form," p. 492-B.

boxes labelled "permission received from copyright owner" and "copying royalty fee paid."[119]

The language suggested by the Register of Copyrights is preferable to ALA's because it would clarify the requesting library's basis for authorization to receive the copy or phonorecord. Under ALA's current form, it is inaccurate to state that the request complies with "other provisions of copyright law" if the copying is authorized, not by section 107 or 108, but by written permission or by payment of royalty.

MULTIPLE COPIES FOR LIBRARY RESERVE AND CLASSROOM USE

Reserve Collections

Academic and school libraries are frequently asked to place certain copyrighted materials on reserve. If the actual books or periodicals are placed on reserve, there is no problem with compliance with copyright provisions. Usually, however, faculty wish to place on reserve multiple copies of copyrighted materials (for example, periodical articles, chapters from books, short stories, poems, etc.). Many academic libraries attempt to deal with this potential problem by requiring "faculty members to vouch for the non-infringing status of photocopies which are placed on reserve."[120] In the case of an infringement, however, it is possible that the faculty member's "voucher" would not absolve the library of liability as a co-infringer.

To assist libraries in determining acceptable reserve collection practices, ALA developed *Model Policy Concerning College and University Photocopying for Classroom Research and Library Reserve Use* (1982). The *Model Policy* indicates that single copies will be placed on reserve for an entire article, chapter, or poem. Multiple copies will be placed on reserve if they meet four criteria:

1. the amount of material should be reasonable in relation

---

119 *Report of the Register of Copyrights* (January, 1983), p. 137.

120 *Report of the Register of Copyrights* (January, 1983), p. 196. For examples of policies see: Indiana University, "Copyright information and guidelines," *University copyright policies in ARL institutions, SPEC Flyer #138* (October, 1987), p. 16. See also, North Carolina State Univ., "Copyright compliance policies," *Photocopying Services in ARL Libraries, SPEC #115* (June, 1985), p. 7.

to the total amount of the material assigned for one term of a course taking into account the nature of the course, its subject matter and level, 17 U.S.C. [section]107(1) and (3);

2. the number of copies should be reasonable in light of the number of students enrolled, the difficulty and timing of assignments, and the number of other courses which may assign the same material, 17 U.S.C. [section] 107(1) and (3);

3. the material should contain a notice of copyright, *see* 17 U.S.C. [section] 401;

4. the effect of photocopying the material should not be detrimental to the market for the work. (In general, the library should own at least one copy of the work.) 17 U.S.C. [section] 107(4).[121]

The *Model Policy* indicates that "less than six" will probably be a reasonable number, but that more may be permitted in unusual circumstances. For example, it is common for large universities to register several hundred students in undergraduate courses. In the case of a class of three hundred students, a larger number of copies would be "reasonable," as "less than six" would clearly be insufficient. The *Model Policy* also advocates obtaining the copyright holder's permission if there is doubt regarding fair use. One authority advocates up to one copy per ten students in the class.[122]

Multiple Copies for Classroom Use

Some academic and school libraries may be asked to provide multiple photocopies of copyrighted materials for classroom use. The fair use guidelines, "II. Multiple Copies for Classroom Use," provide that multiple copies may be made for or by a teacher for classroom use or discussion if they do not exceed more than one copy per pupil in a course, if they meet the tests for brevity, spontaneity, and cumulative

121 American Library Assn., *Model policy concerning college and university photocopying for classroom research and library reserve use* (Chicago: ALA, 1982), p. 6. This policy has been adopted by some libraries; for example, see *Univ. copyright policies in ARL Inst., SPEC #138*, p. 45.
122 Charles W. Vlcek, *Adoptable copyright policy.*

effect, and if each copy includes a notice of copyright.[123] The tests for brevity, spontaneity, and cumulative effect are as follows:

Brevity

(i) Poetry: (a) A complete poem if less than 250 words and if printed on not more than two pages or, (b) from a longer poem, an excerpt of not more than 250 words.

(ii) Prose: (a) Either a complete article, story or essay of less than 2,500 words, or (b) an excerpt from any prose work of not more than 1,000 words or 10% of the work, whichever is less, but in any event a minimum of 500 words.[124]

(iii) Illustration: One chart, graph, diagram, drawing, cartoon or picture per book or per periodical issue.

(iv) "Special" works: Certain works in poetry, prose or in "poetic prose" which often combine language with illustrations and which are intended sometimes for children and at other times for a more general audience fall short of 2,500 words in their entirety. Paragraph "ii" above notwithstanding such "special works" may not be reproduced in their entirety; however, an excerpt comprising not more than two of the published pages of such special work and containing not more then [sic] 10% of the words found in the text thereof, may be reproduced.

Spontaneity

(i) The copying is at the instance and inspiration of the individual teacher, and

(ii) The inspiration and decision to use the work and the moment of its use for maximum teaching effectiveness are so close in time that it would be unreasonable to expect a timely reply to a request for permission.

---

123 H.R. Rep. No. 1476, section 107, in *The official fair use guidelines*, 4th ed., p. 6.

124 Each of the numerical limits stated in "i" and "ii" above may be expanded to permit the completion of an unfinished line of a poem or of an unfinished prose paragraph.

Cumulative Effect

(i) The copying of the material is for only one course in the school in which the copies are made.

(ii) Not more than one short poem, article, story, essay or two excerpts may be copied from the same author, nor more than three from the same collective work or periodical volume during one class term.

(iii) There shall not be more than nine instances of such multiple copying for one course during one class term.

[The limitations stated in "ii" and "iii" above shall not apply to current news periodicals and newspapers and current news sections of other periodicals.][125]

In addition to the tests of brevity, spontaneity, and cumulative effect, the fair use guidelines provide that a student may not be charged beyond the actual cost of the photocopying and that a teacher may not make multiple copies:

(1) to create anthologies, compilations, or collective works;

(2) from "consumable" works, such as workbooks;

(3) to substitute for purchasing books, reprints or periodicals;

(4) at the direction of a higher authority; or

(5) of the same item from term to term.[126]

Not all libraries are in agreement that the fair use guidelines are the "final word" for determining fair use for classroom copying. A major complaint against the fair use guidelines is that, while they may be adequate for K-12 classroom copying, they are not workable for college and university level teaching. This sentiment is clear in ALA's *Model Policy* which states:

These minimum standards normally would not be realistic in the University setting. Faculty members needing to exceed these limits for college education should not feel hampered

---

125 *The official fair use guidelines*, pp. 6–7.
126 *The official fair use guidelines*, pp. 7–8.

by these guidelines, although they should attempt a "selective and sparing" use of photocopied, copyrighted material.

The photocopying practices of an instructor should not have a significant detrimental impact on the market for the copyrighted work. 17 U.S.C. [section] 107(4). To guard against this effect, you usually should restrict use of an item of photocopied material to one course and you should not repeatedly photocopy excerpts from one periodical or author without the permission of the copyright owner.[127]

In spite of ALA's more liberal interpretation of fair use copying for classroom use under section 107, faculty members (and libraries providing multiple copies for faculty) should use extreme caution when venturing beyond the limits set by the fair use guidelines. Periodical publishers have been aggressive in suing for copyright infringement.[128]

To avoid infringement, some universities have entered into photocopying agreements with the Copyright Clearance Center (CCC). Through these agreements, royalties for photocopying from certain journals (beyond what is permitted by sections 107 and 108) are paid to the CCC. For further information, see Chapter Nine.

SUMMARY

Section 108(g) of the Copyright Act of 1976 prohibits "systematic reproduction" of copyrighted materials but permits interlibrary arrangements which do not request such "aggregate quantities" as to substitute for a subscription to or purchase of a work. To assist libraries in applying section 108(g) to interlibrary loan transactions, the Conference adopted the CONTU guidelines.

Instances of multiple copying other than interlibrary loan are addressed in *The Official Fair Use Guidelines*, "Multiple Copies for Classroom Use." Although academic faculty are not enthralled with the fair use guidelines, compliance with the guidelines may protect the college or university against infringement lawsuits. ALA's *Model Policy* pro-

---

127 ALA, *Model policy*, p. 5.
128 For a discussion of recent cases, see for example, James S. Heller and Sarah K. Wiant, *Copyright handbook* (Littleton, CO: AALL, 1984), p. 13-14.

visions for classroom uses are more liberal but are not "officially" recognized.

There are no "official" guidelines for multiple copies for library reserve, but ALA's *Model Policy* presents a workable framework. When in doubt, the wise step is to obtain written permission from the copyright holder.

PART II:

ADDITIONAL COPYRIGHT CONCERNS RELATING TO LIBRARIES

Chapter 7

THE FAIR USE LIMITATION ON EXCLUSIVE RIGHTS

For purposes of introducing librarians and archivists to the concept of "fair use", this Chapter briefly examines the "fair use" limitation on the copyright owner's exclusive rights. The discussion should not be considered conclusive, as indepth coverage would require a full-length book.

FAIR USE UNDER SECTION 107

Librarians should be aware of the basic components of section 107 to differentiate between permissible duplication under section 108 (library photocopying) and section 107 ("fair use"). Section 107 of the Copyright Act of 1976 provides that "fair use" of a copyrighted material is not an infringement of the owner's copyright, even if the use involves one of the five exclusive rights. Section 107 states:

> Notwithstanding the provisions of section 106, the fair use of a copyrighted work, including such use by reproduction in copies of phonorecords or by any other means specified by that section, for purposes such as criticism, comment, news reporting, teaching (including multiple copies for classroom use), scholarship, or research, is not an infringement of copyright. In determining whether the use made of a work in any particular case is a fair use the factors to be considered shall include—
>
> (1) the purpose and character of the use, including whether

such use is of a commercial nature or is for nonprofit educational purposes;

(2) the nature of the copyrighted work;

(3) the amount and substantiality of the portion used in relation to the copyrighted work as a whole; and

(4) the effect of the use upon the potential market for or value of the copyrighted work.[129]

A proposed use must meet all four of the following criteria to qualify as a "fair use" under section 107: (1) purpose and character, (2) nature of the work, (3) amount and substantiality, and (4) effect upon potential market or value of the work.

Purpose and Character

The first criterion requires examination of whether the use is "of a commercial nature or is for nonprofit educational purposes."[130] Acceptable purposes include, but are not limited to, "criticism, comment, news reporting, teaching (including multiple copies for classroom use), scholarship, or research."[131]

Nature of the Work

The second criterion, "nature of the work," indicates that certain works may not qualify for "fair use" due to the type of materials they are. For example, workbooks, by their nature, are meant to be "consumed" by individual students and not to be photocopied. A school could not claim "fair use" if it purchased only one copy of a workbook and then made multiple photocopies for classroom use.

Amount and Substantiality

This criterion refers to the percentage of the work used and how substantial that portion is in relation to the whole. The "Agreement on Guidelines for Classroom Copying in Not-for-Profit Educational Institutions" sets forth tests for brevity, spontaneity, and cumulative effect

---

129 17 U.S.C. 107.
130 17 U.S.C. 107(1).
131 17 U.S.C. 107.

which must be met for a use to conform to the "amount and substantiality" criterion.[132]

"Quantity used" is not, however, the sole factor of the "amount and substantiality" criterion. Even use of a relatively small quantity may not qualify for "fair use" if the portion used is "substantial" in relation to the entire work. In the case of *Folsom v. Marsh*,[133] the court was asked to determine whether the Reverend Charles W. Upham's 866-page *Life of Washington in the Form of an Autobiography* (which included 353 pages taken directly from Jared Sparks' 7,000-pages *Writings of President Washington*) was a fair use. Although 353 pages seemed negligible in proportion to the entire 7,000-page work, the court determined that the portion used was substantial and stated,

> It is certainly not necessary, to constitute an invasion of copyright, that the whole of a work should be copied, or even a large portion of it, in form or in substance. If so much is taken, that the value of the original is sensibly diminished, or the labors of the original author are substantially to an injurious extent appropriated by another, that is sufficient, in point of law, to constitute piracy *pro tanta*. . . . In short, we must often, in deciding questions of this sort, look to the nature and objects of the selections made, the quantity and value of the materials used, and the degree in which the use may prejudice the sale, or diminish the profits, or supersede the objects, of the original work.[134]

The court noted that the pages used were of substantial importance to the *Writings of President Washington* (even though they constituted only a small percentage of the entire work) and enjoined further distribution of Upham's book.

Effect Upon Potential Market or Value of the Work

The test for "effect upon potential market for or value of the copyrighted work" involves determining whether the use will adversely affect the financial interest of the copyright owner. As Dr. Miller explains:

> If a single instance of copying deprives the copyright

---

132 H.R. Rep. No. 1476, Section 107. See Chapter 6 for text and discussion of Guidelines.
133 *Folsom v. Marsh*, 9 Fed. Cas. 342, No. 4901 (C.C.D. Mass. 1841).
134 9 Fed. Cas. at 348.

owner of a legitimate sale, the copying is an infringement of the copyright. Furthermore, if the repeated copying from a work has the cumulative effect of depriving the copyright owner of a sale, that is also infringement.[135]

APPLICATION OF "FAIR USE" TO LIBRARIES

In most instances, libraries and archives will rely on the provisions of section 108 to duplicate materials for patron or library use. There are some instances, however, where a library or archives may make "fair use" copies outside of the provisions of section 108.

For example, if a librarian discovers that two or three pages have been torn out of an encyclopedia volume, fair use would permit the librarian to duplicate and "tip in" the missing pages. If, on the other hand, ninety percent of the pages were torn out or mutilated, it would not be fair use for the librarian to "tip in" copies of those pages. The librarian would either purchase an unused replacement (if available at a fair price) or would rely on the provisions of section 108(c) for duplication of a damaged book (if an unused replacement were unavailable).[136]

As another example, certain copies made for a library's vertical file may constitute fair use duplication. In general, most photocopying for library vertical files is not permitted under section 107 or 108, and libraries should receive permission prior to duplicating copyrighted materials for their vertical files.[137] If the library's copying fits all of the four criteria of section 107, however, the duplication will be fair use. For example, prior to an election a newspaper or journal (subscribed to by the library) publishes an article profiling all of the candidates and issues. There is a high, spontaneous demand for the article during the few days prior to the election, but there is not time for the library to gain written permission to duplicate. It would likely be fair use for the library to make additional copies of the article for placement in the ver-

---

135 Jerome K. Miller, "The duplication of audiovisual materials in libraries," in John Shelton Lawrence and Bernard Timberg, eds., *Fair use and free inquiry* (Norwood, NJ: Ablex Pub. 1980), p. 134.

136 17 U.S.C. 108(c). See Chapter 4 for a detailed discussion of this subsection.

137 See discussion in Chapter 4 under the heading, "Photocopying for Library Vertical Files."

tical file during the period of high demand. After the demand has died down, the library should either destroy the copies or should obtain written permission to retain them in the file.

Another example of libraries' fair use duplication involves school and academic libraries which may be called upon to make multiple copies for classroom or reserve use. Such duplication is fair use if it conforms to the guidelines for section 107. See discussion in Chapter Six, "Multiple Copies for Library Reserve and Classroom Use."

SUMMARY

Section 107 provides that certain uses of copyrighted materials are permissible, and thus "fair use," if they meet the four criteria of (1) purpose and character of use, (2) nature of the work, (3) amount and substantiality of the portion used, and (4) the effect of the use upon the potential market for or value of the work.

Although most duplication by libraries and archives falls under the provisions of section 108, some copying for vertical files or for "tipping in" pages may be fair use under section 107.

Chapter 8

ADDITIONAL LIMITATIONS ON EXCLUSIVE RIGHTS

In addition to sections 108 and 107, sections 109-117 of the Copyright Act of 1976 contain several limitations on the exclusive rights described in section 106. These limitations are separate and distinct from the exemptions of section 107 (fair use) and section 108 (library duplication). This chapter provides a brief overview of several exemptions but should not be considered exhaustive, as an indepth coverage of these exemptions requires a full-length book.

EXEMPTIONS FOR PUBLIC PERFORMANCES AND DISPLAYS

Section 110(1) limits the rights of public performance and of public display by permitting nonprofit educational institutions to display or perform works if certain educational criteria are met. The performance or display must be:

(1) presented by instructors or pupils;

(2) in the course of face-to-face teaching activities;

(3) in a classroom or similar place devoted to instruction (which includes the school library or media center); and

(4) by means of a lawfully-made copy, if the performance or display is of a motion picture or other audiovisual method (or,

73

if not lawfully-made, the presenter must have no reason to know or believe the copy was not lawfully-made).[138]

Section 110(2) permits the transmission of a nondramatic literary or musical work or display of a work by a governmental body or non-profit educational institution if the performance or display is a regular part of the systematic instructional activities and is directly related and of material assistance to the teaching content of the transmission. The transmission must be made primarily for reception:

(1) in classrooms or similar places devoted to instruction;

(2) by disabled persons or others whose circumstances do not permit their attendance in the place of instruction; or

(3) by officers or employees of governmental bodies as part of their official duties or employment.[139]

By definition, section 110(2) excludes performances of dramatic works.

Section 110(3) permits public performances or displays of non-dramatic literary or musical works or dramatico-musical works of a religious nature "in the course of services at a place of worship or other religious assembly."[140] The "course of services" includes regular worship services, as well as special services for religious holidays, weddings, and funerals. A performance or display in a church, synagogue, or other religious building which is not part of the religious services is not covered under section 110(3). Such a performance or display may, however, be permitted under section 110(4).

Section 110(4) permits a public performance of a nondramatic literary or musical work if:

(1) there is no direct or indirect commercial advantage,

(2) there is no payment of a fee or other compensation to the performers, promoters, or organizers, and

(3) there is no admission charge.

---

138 17 U.S.C. 110(1).
139 17 U.S.C. 110(2).
140 17 U.S.C. 110(3).

If there is an admission charge, the proceeds (after deducting reasonable production costs) must be used exclusively for educational, religious, or charitable purposes, and not for private financial gain.[141]

Libraries often present public performances of copyrighted works, such as musical performances, children's storytelling, and poetry readings. Library programming may include performances of copyrighted materials if the abovementioned four criteria of section 110(4) are met. If any of these criteria are not met, however, the library must obtain a performance license from the copyright holder or the appropriate licensing agency to avoid infringement. Libraries which pay outside performers to present library programs should require a written statement indicating that the performer takes the responsiblity for obtaining public performance rights for all copyrighted material used as part of the performance.[142] Dramatic works may not be performed under this section 110(4) exemption. This prohibits the performance of all plays, including "readers theater" and children's plays, without a license. Audiovisual works are also considered "dramatic" works under section 108.

Section 110(4) is unspecific on the question of a library performance presented by paid library personnel. For example, children's storyhour programs are usually conducted by a salaried children's librarian. Because the "performer" is paid, does this mean that the performance is not exempted under section 110(4)? The Senate Report indicates that such performances would be exempted:

> If the performers, directors, or producers of the performance, instead of being paid directly "for the performance," are paid a salary for duties encompassing the performance. Examples are performances by a school orchestra conducted by a music teacher who receives an annual salary.[143]

OTHER EXEMPTIONS

Sections 109-112 and 117 of the Copyright Act of 1976 provide additional limitations on the copyright owner's exclusive rights. Section 109 limits the rights of distribution and of public display by extending

---

141 17 U.S.C. 110(4).
142 See Appendix 11 for a sample form certifying copyright compliance.
143 Sen. Rep. No. 473, p. 77.

these rights, under certain circumstances, to an owner of a lawfully-obtained copy of the work.[144]

Section 111 limits the rights of public performance and of public display by exempting certain secondary transmissions.[145] Under this exemption, hotels, apartment houses, and other similar establishments may relay certain transmissions to guests or residents of the establishment.

Section 112 limits exclusive rights in certain circumstances involving ephemeral recordings which are commonly used by radio stations.[146] With some limitations, section 112 allows a transmitting organization (such as a radio station) to copy a sound recording if used for transmission within its local service area or for archival purposes.

Section 117 permits the owner of a copy of a computer program to make another copy of that program.[147] The new copy must either be (1) created as an essential step in the utilization of the program, or (2) for archival purposes.

OBTAINING PERMISSION

If the use of copyrighted material does not fall under one of the limitations set forth in sections 107-117, then the use is an infringement unless the copyright owner specifically authorizes the use. This permission may be obtained in writing directly from the owner or through a clearance center, such as the Copyright Clearance Center, The Harry Fox Agency, Television Licensing Center, or Copyright Sharing Corporation. Methods of obtaining permission are covered in detail in Chapter Nine of this book.

SUMMARY

Section 110 provides exemptions for certain public performances and displays. Some public performances in libraries are exempted under section 110(4) if: (1) there is no direct or indirect commercial advantage, (2) there is no payment of compensation to performers or others, and (3) there is no admission charge or proceeds are used exclusively for

---

144 17 U.S.C. 109.
145 17 U.S.C. 111.
146 17 U.S.C. 112.
147 17 U.S.C. 117.

educational, religious, or charitable purposes. This exemption does not apply to dramatic or audiovisual works.

Sections 109 and 111–117 of the Copyright Act of 1976 provide additional limitations on the copyright owner's exclusive rights.

If a use of copyrighted materials does not fall within any of the exemptions, written permission must be obtained from the owner or a clearinghouse to avoid copyright infringement. See Chapter Nine regarding obtaining permission.

Chapter 9

OBTAINING PERMISSION

If copying a copyrighted work does not fall within the section 107 or 108 exceptions (or any other exceptions to the author's exclusive rights), the user must obtain permission prior to copying or performing the material. Permission may be obtained directly from the copyright owner or through a licensing agency, such as the Copyright Clearance Center.

WHY REQUEST PERMISSION TO DUPLICATE?

Librarians often encounter users who cannot understand why they must obtain permission to copy materials. They feel that their "need" outweighs any proprietary claim of the copyright owner and that the possibility of criminal prosecution or a civil law suit is highly unlikely. In these situations, the librarian must explain the reasoning for requesting written permission. A good, written, institutional policy which establishes specific procedures for copyright compliance is helpful in this process.

For example, a school librarian responsible for photocopying classroom materials may clash with a teacher who repeatedly requests multiple copies of a particular short story each semester, but who refuses to write for permission. The teacher's argument is that he or she "needs" this particular short story to teach a literature class and that it is not his or her fault that the story has been eliminated from the textbook. The teacher also may argue that time does not permit requesting permission and that the copyright holder may be difficult to locate. The teacher may also argue (incorrectly) that repeated use is a "fair use" under section 107. Without a written school policy delineating the procedure for duplicating copyrighted materials (or without backing of the administration), the librarian may have some difficulty convincing the teacher of the legal necessity of obtaining permission.[148]

Although a teacher or other user may not respond favorably to an explanation of the copyright law, he or she may have more sympathy for the concept when the right of reproduction is explained as a property right. The section 106 exclusive rights are legal property rights, even though the property is intangible, and are commonly called "intellectual property." Like tangible real or personal property rights, the owner controls the use of the property (with some exceptions) and has the sole authority to grant other uses of the property.

Unauthorized use of another's copyrighted material is an infringement, similar to trespass or theft, and permission must be obtained prior to use. The teacher who demands duplication of multiple copies of the same short story year after year may be more willing to take the time to request permission once he or she understands that the infringing use is similar to trespass or theft. That same teacher would probably never "borrow" property from a neighbor without asking permission, no matter how great the need for the item.

WRITING TO THE COPYRIGHT OWNER FOR PERMISSION

When requesting permission from a copyright owner, it is important to remember that the law does not require the copyright owner to grant permission for the proposed use. The owner has the right to refuse to grant permission, and a user denied permission has no legal recourse. If the owner decides to grant permission (with or without conditions), the owner does so as a matter of choice, not as a legal obligation.

When requesting permission, the user should keep in mind that the copyright owner is, in effect, doing the user a favor by granting permission. With this in mind, the user should make the process as easy as possible for the copyright owner by doing the following:

---

148 For an example of a policy designed to be adopted by educational agencies (from kindergarten to graduate schools), see Charles W. Vlcek, *Adoptable copyright policy* (Washington, DC: Association for Educational Communications and Technology, Copyright Information Services, 1992).

1. The request for permission should **always** include a self-addressed stamped envelope for the convenience of the owner. Many large firms will discard the envelope and use their own, but some copyright owners refuse to respond to requests unless a stamped, self-addressed envelope is sent with the request.

2. The user should send **two copies** of the request letter, so that the owner may mail one back and retain the other for his or her files. The request should include spaces at the bottom of the letter for the owner's approval, including signature, date, and conditions (if any). This simplifies the permission process for the owner who may not take the time to write a letter granting permission. Often, corporate copyright holders may respond on their standard copyright permission forms, but others will appreciate the time-saving courtesy.

In addition to the above, the letter[149] requesting permission to duplicate copyrighted material should include the following elements:[150]

1. Author, title, edition, and/or other bibliographic information identifying the material to be duplicated.

2. A clear description of the portion of the item to be duplicated. List the *specific* page numbers, chapters, sections, or articles, or indicate that the entire work will be copied. Include a photocopy, if possible, to facilitate identifying the item to be copied.

3. The purpose of the use. The user should clearly indicate why he or she wishes to duplicate the material. For example, classroom use, inclusion in a newsletter, inclusion in a published anthology, etc.

4. The number of copies to be made.

5. When and how the copies will be distributed. For example, if the copies are for classroom use, the request letter should indicate that the copies will be distributed each semester to all students in the class.

6. The cost (if any) of the distributed material. For example, the letter should indicate if the students will be charged for their copies of the materials and, if so, how much. If the user intends to include the

---

149 See Appendix 10 for sample permission letter.
150 *Report of the Register of Copyrights* (January, 1983), p. 166. See also ALA *Model policy*, p. 7.

material in a published work, the letter should indicate what amount, if any, the user intends to pay the copyright owner.

7. Type of reproduction. For example, photocopy, ditto, microfilm, microfiche, overheads, typeset, videotape, slides, offset, etcetera.

OBTAINING PERMISSION FROM THE COPYRIGHT CLEARANCE CENTER

Many medical, academic, corporate, and other special libraries which do great volumes of photocopying for their patrons find that requesting permission to copy from the copyright owner is inefficient. When the materials are needed quickly (for example, when a hospital library provides multiple copies of journal articles to the staff), there is not always time to wait for written permission from the copyright holder. These libraries find it much more expedient to pay for the use through the Copyright Clearance Center (hereinafter CCC), which has the authority to grant permission for duplication of articles from certain publications.

The CCC was created in 1978 in response to the Senate Report urging the development of "workable clearance and licensing procedures"[151] by the collaborative efforts of the Association of American Publishers, the Authors League, the Industrial Research Institute, and the Information Industry Association.[152] The CCC is a non-profit corporation based in Salem, Massachusetts,[153] which operates a central location for users to receive and to pay for permission to photocopy certain materials. The CCC does not provide actual photocopies but rather acts as an agent for publishers and other copyright holders to streamline granting permission and collecting fees to reproduce copyrighted materials.

The 1983 Report of the Register of Copyrights indicated that librarians were slow to join the CCC for several reasons:

---

151 Sen. Rep. No. 473, p. 71. See also Kathlene Regan & Virginia Riordan, "The Copyright Clearance Center: growing success in the United States towards increasing copyright protection of print publications," *Interlending and Document Supply* 16 (1988): 3.

152 *Report of the Register of Copyrights* (January, 1988), p. 29.

153 Copyright Clearance Center, Inc., 27 Congress Street, Salem, MA 01907, Telephone (508) 744-3350.

1. It does not provide the document wanted.

2. It does not cover an extensive number of titles, and those it does cover are primarily scientific or technical.

3. The recordkeeping is cumbersome, and they would prefer to go directly to the publisher.

4. It costs money, and the publisher, notwithstanding its CCC participation, might grant permission gratis.

5. The photocopying that they do does not require the payment of fees.

6. The fee does not go to the copyright proprietor.[154]

The last "reason" is incorrect, as royalty payments are now paid to registered publishers. During the early stages of the development of the CCC, some publishers surrendered their payments to help cover the CCC's operating and start-up expenses.[155]

The librarians' complaint that the CCC has few titles also is no longer valid. As of 1988, the CCC had more than 75,000 titles, 1,300 publishers, and 2,200 users.[156] The growing success of the CCC is due in part to its offering subscribers the choice of two different services: the "Transactional Reporting Service" and the relatively new "Annual Authorizations Service." It is also due to law suits filed against several major corporations. The suits were all settled out of court, but the concern for future law suits encouraged other users to register with the CCC.

Transactional Reporting Service (TRS)

The Transactional Reporting Service (TRS) was the first service provided by the CCC. Through TRS, libraries and other organizations make the copies, then report the copying to the CCC and pay the copying fees on a copy-by-copy basis.[157] Libraries and other organizations may copy only from titles in their possession and must report each copy made beyond fair use.[158]

---

154 *Report of the Register of Copyrights* (January, 1983), p. 169.
155 Regan, p. 5.
156 *Report of the Register of Copyrights* (January, 1988), p. 30.
157 Regan, p. 4.
158 *Report of the Register of Copyrights* (January, 1988), p. 31.

There are two levels of TRS. Level I (which includes account maintenance, free catalog issues, and retention of copying activity in CCC's database for one year) is available free-of-charge to users who report ninety or more copies every six months and is available for a semiannual fee to low-volume users.[159] Level II (which includes only monthly processing of photocopy reports and distribution of royalties) is available free-of-charge to low-volume users.[160]

Annual Authorizations Service (AAS)

The Annual Authorizations Service (AAS), which began in 1983, provides major corporations with annual, renewable licenses to photocopy from copyrighted materials which are registered with the CCC.[161] The materials must be in the corporation's possession, and the photocopies may only be made for internal use. Distribution of copies to third parties is prohibited.[162] This is a nonintrusive statistical model developed by econometricians from MIT and Harvard which "is based on statistical variables developed by pooling survey data for an *entire industry*."[163] The earlier company-wide survey method, which is used less frequently,

> involves 90-day surveys of photocopy activity at all US sites of a potential licensee. The results of the surveys are multiplied by four to yield a projected annual copying level. The publisher-set fees per copy for each registered title are then applied to those annualized copy estimates to produce a licence price.[164]

The CCC reports that the demand for copyright clearance services is increasing rapidly.[165] The demand will likely remain high if the CCC continues to adapt its services to meet the needs of libraries and others involved in duplication of copyrighted materials.

In addition to the CCC, there are several other licensing agencies for the duplication and performances of music, drama, and videocas-

---

159 Regan, p. 4.
160 Regan, p. 4.
161 Regan, p. 3. See Appendix 12 for sample CCC User License.
162 Regan, p. 3.
163 *Report of the Register of Copyrights* (January, 1988), p. 31.
164 Regan, p. 3-4.
165 Regan, p. 6.

settes. For a complete list of these agencies, see *The Copyright Directory*.[166]

SUMMARY

If a proposed duplication of copyrighted material is not authorized by section 107 or 108, the user must obtain permission from the copyright holder prior to copying the material. Permission may be obtained either by writing directly to the copyright holder or by a license agreement with the Copyright Clearance Center (CCC).

When writing for permission, the user should send two copies of the request letter, together with a stamped, self-addressed envelope for the convenience of the owner. The request letter should include information identifying the material to be copied, the purpose of the use, the number of copies to be made, method of distribution, and cost.

The Copyright Clearance Center (CCC) also grants permission to duplicate certain copyrighted materials. This is done through licenses with individual institutions which submit payment for copies directly to the CCC. The subscribers have the choice of the Annual Authorizations Service or the Transactional Reporting Service.

---

166 *The Copyright Directory: Attorneys, Professors, Government Agencies, Congressional Committees, Searchers, Clearinghouses, Hotlines & Associations, 1990-1991* (Friday Harbor, WA: Copyright Information Services, 1990).

APPENDIX 1

The Gentlemen's Agreement of 1935

The Joint Committee on Materials for Research and the Board of Directors of the National Association of Book Publishers, after conferring on the problem of conscientious observance of copyright that faces research libraries in connection with the growing use of photographic methods of reproduction, have agreed upon the following statement:

> A library, archives office, museum, or similar institution owning books or periodical volumes in which copyright still subsists may make and deliver a single photographic reproduction or reduction of a part thereof to a scholar representing in writing that he desires such reproduction in lieu of loan of such publication or in place of manual transcription and solely for the purposes of research; provided
>
> (1) That the person receiving it is given due notice in writing that he is not exempt from liability to the copyright proprietor for any infringement of copyright by misuse of the reproduction constituting an infringement under the copyright law;
>
> (2) That such reproduction is made and furnished without profit to itself by the institution making it.
>
> The exemption from liability of the library, archives office or museum herein provided for shall extend to every officer, agent or employee of such institution in the making and delivery of such reproduction when acting within the scope of his authority of employment. This exemption for the institution itself carries with it a responsibility to see that library employees caution patrons against the misuse of copyright material reproduced photographically.

Under the law of copyright, authors or their agents are assured of "the exclusive right to print, reprint, publish, copy and vend the copyrighted work," all or part. This means that legally no individual or institution can reproduce by photography or photo-mechanical means, mimeograph or other methods of reproduction a page of any part of a book without the written permission of the owner of the copyright. Society, by law, grants this exclusive right for a term of years in the belief that such exclusive control of creative work is necessary to encourage authorship and scholarship.

While the right of quotation without permission is not provided in law, the courts have recognized the right to a "fair use" of book quotations, the length of a "fair" quotation being dependent upon the type of work quoted from and the "fairness" to the author's interest. Extensive quotation is obviously inimical to the author's interest.

The statutes make no specific provision for a right of a research worker to make copies by hand or by typescript for his research notes, but a student has always been free to "copy" by hand; and mechanical reproductions from copyright materials are presumably intended to take the place of hand transcriptions, and to be governed by the same principles governing hand transcription.

In order to guard against any possible infringement of copyright, however, libraries, archives offices and museums should require each applicant for photo-mechanical reproductions of material to assume full responsibility for such copying, and by his signature to a form printed for the purpose assure the institution that the duplicate being made for him is for his personal use only and is to relieve him of the task of transcription. The form should clearly indicate to the applicant that he is obligated under the law not to use the material thus copied from books for any further reproduction without the express permission of the copyright owner.

It would not be fair to the author or publisher to make possible the substitution of the photostats for the purchase of a copy of the book itself either for an individual library or for any permanent collection in a public or research library. Orders for photo-copying which, by reason of their extensiveness or for any other reasons, violate this principle and should not be accepted. In case of doubt as to whether the excerpt requested complies with this condition, the safe thing to do is to defer action until the owner of the copyright has approved the reproduction.

Out-of-print books should likewise be reproduced only with permission, even if this reproduction is solely for the use of the institution making it and not for sale.

APPENDIX 2

17 U.S.C. 106

106. Exclusive Rights in Copyrighted Works

Subject to sections 107 through 118, the owner of copyright under this title has the exclusive rights to do and to authorize any of the following:

(1) to reproduce the copyrighted work in copies or phonorecords:

(2) to prepare derivative works based upon the copyrighted work;

(3) to distribute copies or phonorecords of the copyrighted work to the public by sale or other transfer of ownership, or by rental, lease, or lending;

(4) in the case of literary, musical, dramatic, and choreographic works, pantomimes, and motion pictures and other audiovisual works, to perform the copyrighted work publicly; and

(5) in the case of literary, musical, dramatic, and choreographic works, pantomimes, and pictorial, graphic, or sculptural works, including the individual images of a motion picture or other audiovisual work, to display the copyrighted work publicly.

APPENDIX 3

17 U.S.C. 107

107. Limitations on Exclusive Rights: Fair Use

Notwithstanding the provisions of section 106, the fair use of a copyrighted work, including such use by reproduction in copies of phonorecords or by any other means specified by that section, for purposes such as criticism, comment, news reporting, teaching (including multiple copies for classroom use), scholarship, or research, is not an infringement of copyright. In determining whether the use made of a work in any particular case is a fair use the factors to be considered shall include—

(1) the purpose and character of the use, including whether such use is of a commercial nature or is for nonprofit educational purposes;

(2) the nature of the copyrighted work;

(3) the amount and substantiality of the portion used in relation to the copyrighted work as a whole; and

(4) the effect of the use upon the potential market for or value of the copyrighted work.

APPENDIX 4

17 U.S.C. 108

108. Limitations on Exclusive Rights: Reproduction by Libraries and Archives

(a) Notwithstanding the provisions of section 106, it is not an infringement of copyright for a library or archives, or any of its employees acting within the scope of their employment, to reproduce no more than one copy or phonorecord, under the conditions specified by this section, if—

    (1) the reproduction or distribution is made without any purpose of direct or indirect commercial advantage;

    (2) the collections of the library or archives are

        (i) open to the public, or

        (ii) available not only to researchers affiliated with the library or archives or with the institutions of which it is a part, but also to other persons doing research in a specialized field; and

    (3) the reproduction or distribution of the work includes a notice of copyright.

(b) The rights of reproduction or distribution under this section apply to a copy or phonorecord of an unpublished work duplicated in facsimile form solely for purposes of preservation and security or for deposit for research use in another library or archives of the type described by clause (2) of sub-section (a), if the copy or phonorecord reproduced is currently in the collections of the library or archives.

(c) The right of reproduction under this section applies to a copy or phonorecord of a published work duplicated in facsimile form solely for the purpose of replacement of a copy or phonorecord that is damaged, deteriorating, lost, or stolen, if the library or archives has, after a reasonable effort, determined that an unused replacement cannot be obtained at a fair price.

(d) The rights of reproduction and distribution under this section apply to a copy, made from the collection of a library or archives where the user makes his or her request or from that of another library or archives, of no more than one article or other contribution to a copyrighted collection or periodical issue, or to a copy or phonorecord of a small part of any other copyrighted work, if—

(1) the copy or phonorecord becomes the property of the user, and the library or archives has had no notice that the copy or phonorecord would be used for any purpose other than private study, scholarship, or research; and

(2) the library or archives displays prominently, at the place where orders are accepted, and includes on its order form, a warning of copyright in accordance with requirements that the Register of Copyrights shall prescribe by regulation.

(e) The rights of reproduction and distribution under this section apply to the entire work, or a substantial part of it, made from the collection of a library or archives where the user makes his or her request or from that of another library or archives, if the library or archives has first determined, on the basis of a reasonable investigation, that a copy or phonorecord of the copyrighted work cannot be obtained at a fair [sic] price, if—

(1) the copy or phonorecord becomes the property of the user, and the library or archives has had no notice that the copy or phonorecord would be used for any purpose other than private study, scholarship, or research; and

(2) the library or archives displays prominently, at the place where orders are accepted, and includes on its order form, a warning of copyright in accordance with requirements that the Register of Copyrights shall prescribe by regulation.

(f) Nothing in this section—

(1) shall be construed to impose liability for copyright infringement upon a library or archives or its employees for the unsupervised use of reproducing equipment located on its premises: *Provided*, That such equipment displays a notice that the making of a copy may be subject to the copyright law;

(2) excuses a person who uses such reproducing equipment or who requests a copy or phonorecord under subsection (d) from liability for copyright infringement for any such act, or for any later use of such copy or phonorecord, if it exceeds fair use as provided by section 107;

(3) shall be construed to limit the reproduction and distribution by lending a limited number of copies and excerpts by a library or archives of an audiovisual news program, subject to clauses (1), (2), and (3) of subsection (a); or

(4) in any way affects the right of fair use as provided by section 107, or any contractual obligations assumed at any time by the library or archives when it obtained a copy or phonorecord of a work in its collections.

(g) The rights of reproduction and distribution under this section extend to the isolated and unrelated reproduction or distribution of a single copy or phonorecord of the same material on separate occasions, but do not extend to cases where the library or archives, or its employee—

(1) is aware or has substantial reason to believe that it is engaging in the related or concerted reproduction or distribution of multiple copies or phonorecords of the same material, whether made on one occasion or over a period of time, and whether intended for aggregate use by one or more individual members of a group; or

(2) engages in the systematic reproduction or distribution of single or multiple copies or phonorecords of material described in subsection (d): *Provided*, That nothing in this clause prevents a library or archives from participating in interlibrary arrangements that do not have, as their purpose or effect, that the library or archives receiving such copies or phonorecords for distribution does so in such aggregate quantities as to substitute for a subscription to or purchase of such work.

(h) The rights of reproduction and distribution under this section do not apply to a musical work, a pictorial, graphic or sculptural work, or a motion picture or other audiovisual work other than an audiovisual work dealing with news, except that no such limitation shall apply with respect to rights granted by subsections (b) and (c), or with respect to pictorial or graphic works published as illustrations, diagrams, or similar adjuncts to works of which copies are reproduced or distributed in accordance with subsections (d) and (e).

(i) Five years from the effective date of this Act, and at five-year intervals thereafter, the Register of Copyrights, after consulting with representatives of authors, book and periodical publishers, and other owners of copyrighted materials, and with representatives of library users and librarians, shall submit to the Congress a report setting forth the extent to which this section has achieved the intended statutory balancing of the rights of creators, and the needs of users. The report should also describe any problems that may have arisen, and present legislative or other recommendations, if warranted.

APPENDIX 5

H.R. Rep. No. 2237, 89th Cong., 2d Sess. (October 12, 1966), pp. 66–67 Section 108. Reproduction of Works in Archival Collections

Although the Committee does not favor special fair use provisions dealing with the problems of library photocopying, it was impressed with the need for a specific exemption permitting reproduction of manuscript collections under certain conditions. Arguments were made by representatives of archivists and historians, the General Services Administration, and the American Council on Education for a statutory provision that would authorize archival institutions to make facsimiles of unpublished works in order to deposit copies in other manuscript collections. They emphasized that the unpublished material in archival collections, which the bill gives statutory protection for the first time, is of little interest to copyright owners but of great historical and scholarly value. They urged that a limited right to duplicate archival collections would not harm the copyright owners' interests but would aid scholarship and enable the storage of security copies at a distance from the originals.

The response to these recommendations was generally sympathetic, and there was little or no opposition to them. The committee has therefore adopted a new provision, section 108, under which a "nonprofit institution, having archival custody over collections of manuscripts, documents, or other unpublished works of value to scholarly research," would be entitled to reproduce "any such work in its collections" under certain circumstances. Only unpublished works could be reproduced under this exemption, but the privilege would extend to any type of work, including photographs, motion pictures, and sound recordings.

The archival reproduction privilege accorded by section 108 would be available only where there was no "purpose of direct or indirect commercial advantage," and where the copies or phonorecords are reproduced in "facsimile." Under the exemption, for example, a repository could make photocopies of manuscripts by microfilm or electrostatic process, but could not reproduce the work in "machine-readable" language for storage in an information system.

The purposes of the reproduction must either be "preservation and security" or "deposit for research use in any other such institution." Thus, no facsimile copies or phonorecords made under this section can be distributed to scholars or the public; if they leave the institution that reproduced them, they must be deposited for research purposes in another "nonprofit institution" that has "archival custody over collections of manuscripts, documents, or other unpublished works of value to scholarly research."

This section is not intended to override any contractual arrangements under which the manuscript material was deposited in the institution. For example, if there is an express contractual prohibition against reproduction for any purpose, section 108 could not be construed as justifying a violation of the contract.

APPENDIX 6

Sen. Rep. No. 473, 94th Cong., 1st Sess. (November 20, 1975), pp. 67–71
Section 108. Reproduction by Libraries and Archives

Notwithstanding the exclusive rights of the owners of copyright, section 108 provides that under certain conditions it is not an infringement of copyright for a library or archives, or any of their employees acting within the scope of their employment, to reproduce or distribute not more than one copy or phonorecord of a work provided (1) the reproduction or distribution is made without any purpose of direct or indirect commercial advantage and (2) the collections of the library or archives are open to the public or available not only to researchers affiliated with the library or archives, but also to other persons doing research in a specialized field, and (3) the reproduction or distribution of the work includes a notice of copyright.

The limitation of section 108 to reproduction and distribution by libraries and archives "without any purpose of direct or indirect commercial advantage" is intended to preclude a library or archives in a profit-making organization from providing photocopies of copyrighted materials to employees engaged in furtherance of the organization's commercial enterprise, unless such copying qualifies as a fair use, or the organization has obtained the necessary copyright licenses. A commercial organization should purchase the number of copies of a work that it requires, or obtain the consent of the copyright owner to the making of the photocopies.

The rights of reproduction and distribution under section 108 apply in the following circumstances:

Archival Reproduction

Subsection (b) authorizes the reproduction and distribution of a copy or phonorecord of an unpublished work duplicated in facsimile form solely for purposes of preservation and security, or for deposit for research use in another library or archives, if the copy or phonorecord reproduced is currently in the collections of the first library or archives. Only unpublished works could be reproduced under this exemption, but the right would extend to any type of work, including photographs, motion pictures and sound recordings. Under this exemption, for example, a repository could make photocopies of manuscripts by microfilm or electrostatic process, but could not reproduce the work in "machine-readable" language for storage in an information system.

Replacement of Damaged Copy

Subsection (c) authorizes the reproduction of a published work duplicated in facsimile form solely for the purpose of replacement of a copy or phonorecord that is damaged, deteriorating, lost, or stolen, if the library or archives has, after a reasonable effort, determined that an unused replacement cannot be obtained at a fair price. The scope and nature of a reasonable investigation to determine that an unused replacement cannot be obtained will vary according to the circumstances of a particular situation. It will always require recourse to commonly-known trade sources in the United States, and in the normal situation also to the published or other copyright owner (if such owner can be located at the address listed in the copyright registration), or an authorized reproducing service.

Articles and Small Excerpts

Subsection (d) authorizes the reproduction and distribution of a copy of not more than one article or other contribution to a copyrighted collection of a periodical or copy or phonorecord of a small part of any other copyrighted work. The copy may be made by the library where the user makes his request or by another library pursuant to an inter-library loan. It is further required that the copy become the property of the user, that the library or archives have no notice that the copy would be used for any purposes other than private study, scholarship or research, and that the library or archives display prominently at the place where reproduction requests are accepted, and includes in its order form, a warning of copyright in accordance with requirements that the Register of Copyrights shall prescribe by regulation.

Out-of-print Works

Subsection (e) authorizes the reproduction and distribution of a copy of a work, with certain exceptions, at the request of the user of the collection if the user has established that an unused copy cannot be obtained at a fair price. The copy may be made by the library where the user makes his request or by another library pursuant to an inter-library loan. The scope and nature of a reasonable investigation to determine that an unused copy cannot be obtained will vary according to the circumstances of a particular situation. It will always require recourse to commonly-known trade sources in the United States, and in the normal situation also to the publisher or other copyright owner (if the owner can be located at the address listed in the copyright registration), or an authorized reproducing service. It is further required that the copy become the property of the user, that the library archives have no notice that the copy would be used for any purpose other than private study, scholarship, or research, and that the library or archives display prominently at the place where reproduction requests are accepted, and included on its order form, a warning of copyright in accordance with requirements that the Register of Copyright shall prescribe by regulation.

General Exemptions

Clause (1) of subsection (f) specifically exempts a library or archives or their employees from such liability provided that the reproducing equipment displays a notice that the making of a copy may be subject to the copyright law. Clause (2) of subsection (f) makes clear that this exemption of the library or archives does not extend to the person using such equipment or requesting such copy if the use exceeds fair use. Insofar as such person is concerned the copy made is not considered "lawfully" made for purposes of sections 109, 110 or other provisions of this title. Clause (3) in addition to asserting that nothing contained in section 108 "affects the right of fair use as provided by section 107," also provides that the right of reproduction granted by this section does not override any contractual arrangements assumed by a library or archives when it obtained a work for its collections. For example, if there is an express contractual prohibition against reproduction for any purpose, this legislation shall not be construed as justifying a violation of the contract. This clause is intended to encompass the situation where an individual makes papers, manuscripts or other works available to a library with the understanding that they will not be reproduced.

Clause (4) provides that nothing in section 108 is intended to limit the reproduction and distribution of a limited number of copies and excerpts of an audiovisual news program.

This clause was first added to the revision bill last year by the adoption of an amendment proposed by Senator Baker. It is intended to permit libraries and archives, subject to the general conditions of this section, to make off-the-air videotape recordings of television news programs. Despite the importance of preserving television news, the United States currently has no institution performing this function on a systematic basis.

The purpose of this clause is to prevent the copyright law from precluding such operations as the Vanderbilt University Television News Archive, which makes videotape recordings of television news programs, prepares indexes of the contents, and leases copies of complete broadcasts or compilations of coverage of specified subjects for limited periods upon request from scholars and researchers.

Because of the important copyright policy issues inherent in this issue, the exemption has been narrowly drafted. The Register of Copyrights in 1974 advised that the language of this clause was technically appropriate for its purpose and not "broader than is necessary to validate the Vanderbilt operation."

The Copyright Office recommended that if the Congress desires a news videotape exemption it should be incorporated in section 108. The Copyright Office stated that the inclusion of such a clause in section 108 would be adequate "to enable the Vanderbilt operation to continue."

It is the intent of this legislation that a subsequent unlawful use by a user of a copy of a work lawfully made by a library, shall not make the library liable for such improper use.

Multiple Copies and Systematic Reproduction

Subsection (g) provides that the rights granted by this section extend only to the "isolated and unrelated reproduction of a single copy," but this section does not authorize the related or concerted reproduction of multiple copies of the same material whether made on one occasion or over a period of time, and whether intended for aggregate use by one individual or for separate use by the individual members of a group. For example, if a college professor instructs his class to read an article from a copyrighted journal, the school library would not be permitted, under subsection (g), to reproduce copies of the article for the members of the class.

Subsection (g) also provides that section 108 does not authorize the systematic reproduction or distribution of copies or phonorecords of articles or other contributions to copyrighted collections or periodicals or of small parts of other copyrighted works whether or not multiple copies are reproduced or distributed. Systematic reproduction or distribution occurs when a library makes copies of such material available to other libraries or to groups of users under formal or informal arrangements whose purpose or effect is to have the reproducing library serve as their source of such material. Such systematic reproduction and distribution, as distinguished from isolated and unrelated reproduction or distribution, may substitute the copies reproduced by the source library for subscriptions or reprints or other copies which the receiving libraries or users might otherwise have purchased for themselves, from the publisher or the licensed reproducing agencies.

While it is not possible to formulate specific definitions of "systematic copying," the following examples serve to illustrate some of the copying prohibited by subsection (g).

(1) A library with a collection of journals in biology informs other libraries with similar collections that it will maintain and build its own collection and will make copies of articles from these journals available to them and their patrons on request. Accordingly, the other libraries discontinue or refrain from purchasing subscriptions to these journals and fulfill their patrons' requests for articles by obtaining photocopies from the source library.

(2) A research center employing a number of scientists and technicians subscribes to one or two copies of needed periodicals. By reproducing photocopies of articles the center is able to make the material in these periodicals available to its staff in

the same manner which otherwise would have required multiple subscriptions.

(3) Several branches of a library system agree that one branch will subscribe to particular journals in lieu of each branch purchasing its own subscriptions, and the one subscribing branch will reproduce copies of articles from the publication for users of the other branches.

The committee believes that section 108 provides an appropriate statutory balancing of the rights of creators, and the needs of users. However, neither a statute nor legislative history can specify precisely which library photocopying practices constitute the making of "single copies" as distinguished from "systematic reproduction." Isolated, single spontaneous requests must be distinguished from "systematic reproduction." The photocopying needs of such operations as multi-county regional systems must be met. The committee therefore recommends that representatives of authors, book and periodical publishers and other owners of copyrighted material meet with the library community to formulate photocopying guidelines to assist library patrons and employees. Concerning library photocopying practices not authorized by this legislation, the committee recommends that workable clearance and licensing procedures by developed.

It is still uncertain how far a library may go under the Copyright Act of 1909 in supplying a photocopy of copyrighted material in its collection. The recent case of *The Williams and Wilkins Company v. The United States* failed to significantly illuminate the application of the fair use doctrine to library photocopying practices. Indeed, the opinion of the Court of Claims said the Court was engaged in "a'holding operation' in the interim period before Congress enacted its preferred solution."

While the several opinions in the *Wilkins* case have given the Congress little guidance as to the current state of the law on fair use, these opinions provide additional support for the balanced resolution of the photocopying issue adopted by the Senate last year in S. 1361 and preserved in section 108 of this legislation. As the Court of Claims opinion succinctly stated "there is much to be said on all sides."

In adopting these provisions on library photocopying, the committee is aware that through such programs as those of the National Commission on Libraries and Information Science there will be a significant evolution in the functioning and services of libraries. To consider the possible need for changes in copyright law and procedures as a result of new technology, a National Commission on New Technological Uses of Copyrighted Works has been established (Public Law 93-573).

Works Excluded

Subsection (h) provides that the rights of reproduction and distribution under this section do not apply to a musical work, a pictorial, graphic or sculptural work, or a motion picture or other audio-visual work. Such limitation does not apply to archival reproduction and replacement of a damaged copy.

APPENDIX 7

H.R. Rep. No. 1476, 94th Cong., 2d Sess. (September 3, 1976), pp. 74–79
Section 108. Reproduction by Libraries and Archives

Notwithstanding the exclusive rights of the owners of copyright, section 108 provides that under certain conditions it is not an infringement of copyright for a library or archives, or any of their employees acting within the scope of their employment, to reproduce or distribute not more than one copy or phonorecord of a work provided (1) the reproduction or distribution is made without any purpose of direct or indirect commercial advantage and (2) the collections of the library or archives are open to the public or available not only to researchers affiliated with the library or archives, but also to other persons doing research in a specialized field, and (3) the reproduction or distribution of the work includes a notice of copyright.

Under this provision, a purely commercial enterprise could not establish a collection of copyrighted works, call itself a library or archive, and engage in for-profit reproduction and distribution of photocopies. Similarly, it would not be possible for a non-profit institution, by means of contractual arrangements with a commercial copying enterprise, to authorize the enterprise to carry out copying and distribution functions that would be exempt if conducted by the non-profit institution itself.

The reference to "indirect commercial advantage" has raised questions as to the status of photocopying done by or for libraries or archival collections within industrial, profitmaking, or proprietary institutions (such as the research and development departments of chemical, pharmaceutical, automobile, and oil corporations, the library of a proprietary hospital, the collections owned by a law or medical partnership, etc.)

There is a direct interrelationship between this problem and the prohibitions against "multiple" and "systematic" photocopying in sec-

107

tion 108(g) (1) and (2). Under section 108, a library in a profit-making organization would not be authorized to:

(a) use a single subscription or copy to supply its employees with multiple copies of material relevant to their work; or

(b) use a single subscription or copy to supply its employees, on request, with single copies of material relevant to their work, where the arrangement is "systematic" in the sense of deliberately substituting photocopying for subscription or purchase; or

(c) use "interlibrary loan" arrangements for obtaining photocopies in such aggregate quantities as to substitute for subscriptions or purchase of material needed by employees in their work.

Moreover, a library in a profit-making organization could not evade these obligations by installing reproducing equipment on its premises for unsupervised use by the organization's staff.

Isolated, spontaneous making of single photocopies by a library in a for-profit organization, without any systematic effort to substitute photocopying for subscriptions or purchases, would be covered by section 108, even though the copies are furnished to the employees of the organization for use in their work.

Similarly, for-profit libraries could participate in interlibrary arrangements for exchange of photocopies, as long as the production or distribution was not "systematic." These activities, by themselves, would ordinarily not be considered "for direct or indirect commercial advantages," since the "advantage" referred to in this clause must attach to the immediate commercial motivation behind the reproduction or distribution itself, rather than to the ultimate profit-making motivation behind the enterprise in which the library is located. On the other hand, section 108 would not excuse reproduction or distribution if there were a commercial motive behind the actual making or distributing of the copies, if multiple copies were made or distributed, or if the photocopying activities were "systematic" in the sense that their aim was to substitute for subscriptions or purchases.

Archival Reproduction

Subsection (b) authorizes the reproduction and distribution of a copy or phonorecord of an unpublished work duplicated in facsimile form solely for purposes of preservation and security, or for deposit for research use in another library or archives, if the copy or phonorecord reproduced is currently in the collections of the first library or archives. Only unpublished works could be reproduced under this exemption, but the right would extend to any type of work, including photographs, motion pictures and sound recordings. Under this exemption, for example, a repository could make photocopies of manuscripts by microfilm or electrostatic process, but could not reproduce the work in "machine-readable" language for storage in an information system.

Replacement of Damaged Copy

Subsection (c) authorizes the reproduction of a published work duplicated in facsimile form solely for the purpose of replacement of a copy or phonorecord that is damaged, deteriorating, lost, or stolen, if the library or archives has, after a reasonable effort, determined that an unused replacement cannot be obtained at a fair price. The scope and nature of a reasonable investigation to determine that an unused replacement cannot be obtained will vary according to the circumstances of a particular situation. It will always require recourse to commonly-known trade sources in the United States, and in the normal situation also to the publisher or other copyright owner (if such owner can be located at the address listed in the copyright registration), or an authorized reproducing service.

Articles and Small Excerpts

Subsection (d) authorizes the reproduction and distribution of a copy of not more than one article or other contribution to a copyrighted collection of a periodical or copy or phonorecord of a small part of any other copyrighted work. The copy may be made by the library where the user makes his request or by another library pursuant to an inter-library loan. It is further required that the copy become the property of the user, that the library or archives have no notice that the copy would be used for any purposes other than private study, scholarship or research, and that the library or archives display prominently at the place where reproduction requests are accepted, and includes in its order form, a warning of copyright in accordance with requirements that the Register of Copyrights shall prescribe by regulation.

Out-of-print Works

Subsection (e) authorizes the reproduction and distribution of a copy of a work, with certain exceptions, at the request of the user of the collection if the user has established that an unused copy cannot be obtained at a fair price. The copy may be made by the library where the user makes his request or by another library pursuant to an inter-library loan. The scope and nature of a reasonable investigation to determine that an unused copy cannot be obtained will vary according to the circumstances of a particular situation. It will always require recourse to commonly-known trade sources in the United States, and in the normal situation also to the publisher or other copyright owner (if the owner can be located at the address listed in the copyright registration), or an authorized reproducing service. It is further required that the copy become the property of the user, that the library archives have no notice that the copy would be used for any purpose other than private study, scholarship, or research, and that the library or archives display prominently at the place where reproduction requests are accepted, and included on its order form, a warning of copyright in accordance with requirements that the Register of Copyright shall prescribe by regulation.

General Exemptions

Clause (1) of subsection (f) specifically exempts a library or archives or its employees from liability for the unsupervised use of reproducing equipment located on its premises, provided that the reproducing equipment displays a notice that the making of a copy may be subject to the copyright law. Clause (2) of subsection (f) makes clear that this exemption of the library or archives does not extend to the person using such equipment or requesting such copy if the use exceeds fair use. Insofar as such person is concerned the copy made is not considered "lawfully" made for purposes of sections 109, 110 or other provisions of this title.

Clause (3) provides that nothing in section 108 is intended to limit the reproduction and distribution by lending of a limited number of copies and excerpts of an audiovisual news program. This exemption is intended to apply to the daily newscasts of the national television networks, which report the major events of the day. It does not apply to documentary (except documentary programs involving news reporting as that term is used in section 107), magazine-format or other public affairs broadcasts dealing with subjects of general interest to the viewing public.

The clause was first added to the revision bill in 1974 by the adoption of an amendment proposed by Senator Baker. It is intended to permit libraries and archives, subject to the general conditions of this section, to make off-the-air videotape recordings of daily network newscasts for limited distribution to scholars and researchers for use in research purposes. As such, it is an adjunct to the American Television and Radio Archive established in Section 113 of the Act which will be the principal repository for television broadcast material, including news broadcasts. The inclusion of language indicating that such material may only be distributed by lending by the library or archive is intended to preclude performance, copying, or sale, whether or not for profit, by the recipient of a copy of a television broadcast taped off-the-air pursuant to this clause.

Clause (4), in addition to asserting that nothing contained in section 108 "affects the right of fair use as provided by section 107," also provides that the right of reproduction granted by this section does not override any contractual arrangements assumed by a library or archives when it obtained a work for its collections. For example, if there is an express contractual prohibition against reproduction for any purpose, this legislation shall not be construed as justifying a violation of the contract. This clause is intended to encompass the situation where an individual makes papers, manuscripts or other works available to a library with the understanding that they will not be reproduced.

It is the intent of this legislation that a subsequent unlawful use by a user of a copy or phonorecord of a work lawfully made by a library, shall not make the library liable for such improper use.

Multiple Copies and Systematic Reproduction

Subsection (g) provides that the rights granted by this section extend only to the "isolated and unrelated reproduction of a single copy or phonorecord of the same material on separate occasions." However, this section does not authorize the related or concerted reproduction of

111

multiple copies or phonorecords of the same materials, whether made on one occasion or over a period of time, and whether intended for aggregate use by one individual or for separate use by the individual members of a group.

With respect to material described in subsection (d)—articles or other contributions to periodicals or collections, and small parts of other copyrighted works—subsection (g)(2) provides that the exemptions of section 108 do not apply if the library or archive engages in "systematic reproduction or distribution of single or multiple copies or phonorecords." This provision in S. 22 provoked a storm of controversy, centering around the extent to which the restrictions on "systematic" activities would prevent the continuation and development of interlibrary networks and other arrangements involving the exchange of photocopies. After thorough consideration, the Committee amended section 108(g)(2) to add the following proviso:

> *Provided*, that nothing in this clause prevents a library or archives from participating in interlibrary arrangements that do not have, as their purpose or effect, that the library or archives receiving such copies or phonorecords for distribution does so in such aggregate quantities as to substitute for a subscription to or purchase of such work.

In addition, the Committee added a new subsection (i) to section 108, requiring the Register of Copyrights, five years from the effective date of the new Act and at five-year intervals thereafter, to report to Congress upon "the extent to which this section has achieved the intended statutory balancing of the rights of creators, and the needs of users," and to make appropriate legislative or other recommendations. As noted in connection with section 107, the Committee also amended section 504(c) in a way that would insulate librarians from unwarranted liability for copyright infringement; this amendment is discussed below.

The key phrases in the Committee's amendment of section 108(g)(2) are "aggregate quantities" and "substitute for a subscription to or purchase of" a work. To be implemented effectively in practice, these provisions will require the development and implementation of more-or-less specific guidelines establishing criteria to govern various situations.

The National Commission on New Technological Uses of Copyrighted Works (CONTU) offered to provide good offices in helping to develop these guidelines. This offer was accepted and, although the final text of guidelines has not yet been achieved, the Committee has reason to hope that, within the next month, some agreement can be reached on an initial set of guidelines covering practices under section 108(g)(2).

Works Excluded

Subsection (h) provides that the rights of reproduction and distribution under this section do not apply to a musical work, a pictorial, graphic or sculptural work, or a motion picture or other audiovisual work other than "an audiovisual work dealing with the news." The latter term is intended as the equivalent in meaning of the phrase "audiovisual news program" in section 108(f)(3). The exclusions under subsection (h) do not apply to archival reproduction under subsection (b), to replacement of damaged or lost copies or phonorecords under subsection (c), or to "pictorial or graphic works published as illustrations, diagrams, or similar adjuncts to works of which copies are reproduced or distributed in accordance with subsections (d) and (e)."

Although subsection (h) generally removes musical, graphic, and audiovisual works from the specific exemptions of section 108, it is important to recognize that the doctrine of fair use under section 107 remains fully applicable to the photocopying or other reproduction of such works. In the case of music, for example, it would be fair use for a scholar doing musicological research to have a library supply a copy of a portion of a score or to reproduce portions of a phonorecord of a work. Nothing in section 108 impairs the applicability of the fair use doctrine to a wide variety of situations involving photocopying of other reproduction by a library of copyrighted material in its collections, where the user requests the reproduction for legitimate scholarly or research purposes.

APPENDIX 8

H.R. Rep. No. 1733, 94th Cong., 2d Sess. (September 29, 1976), pp. 71–74 [CONTU Guidelines] Reproduction by Libraries and Archives

Senate Bill

Section 108 of the Senate bill dealt with a variety of situations involving photocopying and other forms of reproduction by libraries and archives. It specified the conditions under which single copies of copyrighted material can be noncommercially reproduced and distributed, but made clear that the privileges of a library or archives under the section do not apply where the reproduction or distribution is of multiple copies or is "systematic." Under subsection (f), the section was not to be construed as limiting the reproduction and distribution, by a library or archive meeting the basic criteria of the section, of a limited number of copies and excerpts of an audiovisual news program.

House Bill

The House bill amended section 108 to make clear that, in cases involving interlibrary arrangements for the exchange of photocopies, the activity would not be considered "systematic" as long as the library or archives receiving the reproductions for distribution does not do so in such aggregate quantities as to substitute for a subscription to or purchase of the work. A new subsection (i) directed the Register of Copyrights, by the end of 1982 and at five-year intervals thereafter, to report on the practical success of the section in balancing the various interests, and to make recommendations for any needed changes. With respect to audiovisual news programs, the House bill limited the scope of the distribution privilege confirmed by section 108(f)(3) to cases where the distribution takes the form of a loan.

Conference Substitute

The conference substitute adopts the provision of section 108 as amended by the House bill. In doing so, the conferees have noted two letters dated September 22, 1976, sent respectively to John L. McClellan, Chairman of the Senate Judiciary Subcommittee on Patents, Trademarks, and Copyrights, and to Robert W. Kastenmeier, Chairman of the House Judiciary Subcommittee on Courts, Civil Liberties, and the Administration of Justice. The letters, from the Chairman of the National Commission on New Technological Uses of Copyrighted Works (CONTU), Stanley H. Fuld, transmitted a document consisting of "guidelines interpreting the provision in subsection (g)(2) of S. 22, as approved by the House Committee on the Judiciary." Chairman Fuld's letters explain that, following lengthy consultations with the parties concerned, the Commission adopted these guidelines as fair and workable and with the hope that conferees on S. 22 may find that they merit inclusion in the conference report. The letters add that, although time did not permit securing signatures of the representatives of the principal library organizations or of the organizations representing publishers and authors on these guidelines, the Commission had received oral assurances from these representatives that the guidelines are acceptable to their organizations.

The conference committee understands that the guidelines are not intended as, and cannot be considered, explicit rules or directions governing any and all cases, now or in the future. It is recognized that their purpose is to provide guidance in the most commonly-encountered interlibrary photocopying situations, that they are not intended to be limiting or determinative in themselves or with respect to other situations, and that they deal with an evolving situation that will undoubtedly require their continuous reevaluation and adjustment. With these qualifications, the conference committee agrees that the guidelines are a reasonable interpretation of the proviso of section 108(g)(2) in the most common situations to which they apply today.

The text of the guidelines follows:

PHOTOCOPYING—INTERLIBRARY ARRANGEMENTS

Introduction

Subsection 108(g)(2) of the bill deals, among other things, with limits on interlibrary arrangements for photocopying. It prohibits systematic photocopying of copyrighted materials but permits interlibrary arrangements "that do not have, as their purpose or effect, that the library or archives receiving such copies or phonorecords for distribution does so in such aggregate quantities as to substitute for a subscription to or purchase of such work."

The National Commission on New Technological Uses of Copyrighted Works offered its good offices to the House and Senate subcommittees in bringing the interested parties together to see if agreement could be reached on what a realistic definition would be of "such aggregate quantities." The Commission consulted with the parties and suggested the interpretation which follows, on which there has been substantial agreement by the principal library, publisher, and author organizations. The Commission considers the guidelines which follow to be a workable and fair interpretation of the intent of the proviso portion of subsection 108(g)(2).

These guidelines are intended to provide guidance in the application of section 108 to the most frequently encountered interlibrary case of a library's obtaining from another library, in lieu of interlibrary loan, copies of articles from relatively recent issues of periodicals—these published within five years prior to the date when the request for the copy thereof is made, constitutes a substitute for a subscription to such periodical. The meaning of the proviso to subsection 108(g)(2) in such case is left to future interpretation.

The point has been made that the present practice on interlibrary loans and use of photocopies in lieu of loans may be supplemented or even largely replaced by a system in which one or more agencies or institutions, public or private, exist for the specific purpose of providing a central source for photocopies. Of course, these guidelines would not apply to such a situation.

GUIDELINES FOR THE PROVISO OF SUBSECTION 108(G)(2)

1. As used in the proviso of subsection 108(g)(2), the words ". . . such aggregate quantities as to substitute for a subscription to or purchase of such work" shall mean:

   (a) with respect to any given periodical (as opposed to any given

117

issue of a periodical), filled requests of a library or archives (a "requesting entity") within any calendar year for a total of six or more copies of an article or articles published in such periodical within five years prior to the date of the request. These guidelines specifically shall not apply, directly or indirectly, to any request of a requesting entity for a copy or copies of an article or articles published in any issue of a periodical, the publication date of which is more than five years prior to the date when the request is made. These guidelines do not define the meaning, with respect to such a request, of ". . . such aggregate quantities as to substitute for a subscription to [such periodical]."

(b) With respect to any other material described in subsection 108(d), (including fiction and poetry), filled requests of a requesting entity within any calendar year for a total of six or more copies or phonorecords of or from any given work (including a collective work) during the entire period when such material shall be protected by copyright.

2. In the event that a requesting entity—

(a) shall have in force or shall have entered an order for a subscription to a periodical, or

(b) has within its collection, or shall have entered an order for, a copy or phonorecord of any other copyrighted work, material from either category of which it desires to obtain by copy of another library or archives (the "supplying entity"), because the material to be copied is not reasonably available for use by the requesting entity itself, then the fulfillment of such request shall be treated as though the requesting entity made such copy from its own colleciton. A library or archives may request a copy or phonorecord from a supplying entity only under those circumstances where the requesting entity would have been able, under the other provisions of section 108, to supply such copy from materials in its own collection.

3. No request for a copy or phonorecord of any material to which these guidelines apply may be fulfilled by the supplying entity unless such request is accompanied by a representation by the requesting entity that the request was made in conformity with these guidelines.

4. The requesting entity shall maintain records of all requests made by it for copies or phonorecords of any materials to which these guidelines apply and shall maintain records of the fulfillment of such requests, which records shall be retained until the end of the third complete calendar year after the end of the calendar year in which the respective request shall have been made.

5. As part of the review provided for in subsection 108(i), these guidelines shall be reviewed not later than five years from the effective date of this bill.

The conference committee is aware that an issue has arisen as to the meaning of the phrase "audiovisual news program" in section 108(f)(3). The conferees believe that, under the provision as adopted in the conference substitute, a library or archives qualifying under section 108(a) would be free, without regard to the archival activities of the Library of Congress or any other organization, to reproduce, on videotape or any other medium of fixation or reproduction, local, regional, or network newscasts, interviews concerning current news events, and on-the-spot coverage of news events, and to distribute a limited number of reproductions of such a program on a loan basis.

Another point of interpretation involves the meaning of "indirect commercial advantage," as used in section 108(a)(1), in the case of libraries or archival collections within industrial, profit-making, or proprietary institutions. As long as the library or archives meets the criteria in section 108(a) and the other requirements of the section, including the prohibitions against multiple and systematic copying in subsection (g), the conferees consider that the isolated, spontaneous making of single photocopies by a library or archives in a for-profit organization without any commercial motivation, or participation by such a library or archives in interlibrary arrangements, would come within the scope of section 108.

APPENDIX 9

Sample Access Policy (For Private Libraries Which Are "Open to the Public")

The XYZ Corporation Library is open to all employees between 8:00 am and 6:00 pm on weekdays (regular working hours) and on weekends with special permission of the librarian.

Non-employees are guaranteed access to the Corporation Library subject to the following conditions:

(1) Non-employees may not use the Library without an appointment. Appointments may be made by calling the librarian during regular working hours.

(2) Only persons eighteen or older may use the library.

(3) Non-employees are not permitted access to the Corporation's database, nor to designated private research files.

(4) Non-employees may use the library from 10:00 am to 5:00 p.m. on the scheduled appointment day. If additional time is necessary, further appointments must be scheduled with the librarian.

(5) To ensure adequate working space for employees, no more than five non-employees may obtain appointments to use the Library in a single business day. Appointments are determined on a "first-come, first-served" basis.

APPENDIX 10

Sample Permission Letter

Dear Author:

I would like permission to reproduce your article, "How to Get Your Friends of the Library to Raise Money," *Library Friends Quarterly* (May, 1991), pp. 5-7, in our library's monthly newsletter. The newsletter is mailed free-of-charge to all library cardholders (approximately 2,850 people). A sample copy of our newsletter is enclosed.

Enclosed for your convenience is a self-addressed stamped envelope and an additional copy of this letter for your files. Please feel free to contact me if you have questions.

Thank you for your consideration of our request.

Sincerely,

Librarian

enc.

Permission Granted _____ Denied_____

Signature _____

Date _____

Conditions (if any) _____

_____

APPENDIX 11

Sample Form For Certification of Copyright Compliance (For Performers Using Copyrighted Materials in Library Programs)

I, _____ (name), certify that I have obtained copyright permission to perform publicly the following works which I will include in my performance for the Library on _____ (date):

[list of copyrighted works]

I hereby take full responsibility for complying with the copyright law during my performance. The library is not liable for any copyright infringements I may commit during my performance.

Signed _____

Date _____

APPENDIX 12

CCC User License

WHEREAS, the Copyright Clearance Center ("CCC") is organized and existing under the New York Not-for-Profit Corporation Law and was established in response to the suggestion of Congress that workable clearance and licensing procedures be created to facilitate authorizations to reproduce copyrighted works; and

WHEREAS,_____("User") is a for-profit commercial or industrial corporation and desires to utilize CCC as a clearance center through which it will be licensed on an annual basis at the premises listed in the annexed Schedule C to reproduce, upon payment of fees, copies of parts of the works listed in the annexed Schedule A, for its internal use and not for distribution to third parties.

NOW, THEREFORE, in furtherance of such objectives, User and CCC hereby agree as follows:

1. CCC, as an agent of the Publishers listed in Schedule A, hereby grants to User a non-exclusive license to reproduce articles or chapters (or portions thereof) from each of the works listed in Schedule A, upon payment to CCC of the license fees set forth in the annexed Schedule B, calculated for each of the premises listed in Schedule C. The Schedule B license fees have been computed by CCC by reference to the schedule of fees established by each Publisher with respect to each work, as set forth in Schedule A, and based upon the extent of User's copying activities at each of the premises with respect to particular works, as determined pursuant to the sampling procedures mentioned in Paragraph 5 below. User will notify CCC promptly of any change at any licensed premises that might reasonably be expected significantly to affect User's requirements and conditions relating to the copying of particular works that are set forth below.

2. No payment is sought or required hereunder with respect to the copying from any works for which other licensing arrangements for authorized copying have been made by or on behalf of User with the copyright proprietors of such works or on their behalf. To the extent that a Publisher whose works are licensed hereunder has determined to make

an allowance against fees payable with respect to the copying of any of its works listed in Schedule A to take account of copies for which payment will not be required because of one or more of various factors, including fair use, such allowance is set forth in Schedule A hereof and has been incorporated into the license fees computed and set forth in Schedule B hereof.

3.1. The reproduction rights granted by the Agreement are limited to the right to make copies in paper form or in microform solely for User's internal use and not for distribution to third parties of individual articles or chapters (or parts thereof) from the works as originally published or copies thereof in paper form or in microform. The license does not grant any rights to input into or store in any computer or other device any part of a work, except for the sole purpose of making an identical paper copy or microform immediately after such input, unless provision has been made in the sampling procedures with respect to User to account for other processes by which identical paper copies or microforms are produced. Nor does this license grant any right to create a data base from any work or to produce any non-identical copies of any work.

3.2. The rights granted hereunder do not extend to User's request for or receipt of copies of the works listed in Schedule A from outside sources, within or outside the United States, whether through "interlibrary arrangements" or from document-supply sources or otherwise. As to such copies User remains obligated to obtain authorizations separate from this licensing system, e.g., through payment of the stated transactional copying royalty established by a Publisher for such reproduction through the CCC transactional reporting system or through the copy supplier.

4. The rights granted hereunder further do not include any rights to copy a work in its entirety. For purposes of this Paragraph, each issue of a journal or other periodical shall be considered a separate work.

5. CCC has ascertained the extent of User's copying activities through statistical means based on the photocopying activity of industries reasonably congruent to User's business activities and User's employee configuration. User agrees to cooperate with CCC in conducting a sampling of User's photocopying activities of 60 days' duration, at up to two User company locations which are mutually agreed upon by the parties, to commence within 90 days after the effective date of the

License. User agrees to bear the costs of the sampling, not to exceed $5,000. The parties agree that the sampling may have to be redone if CCC determines that the sampling(s) conducted did not comply with CCC's standard procedures then in effect; User agrees to bear any attendant additional costs.

Each of the Publishers whose works are licensed hereunder has agreed with CCC to rely upon results of any sampling as well as any other data supplied by User for computing the amount of License fees pertaining thereto. In agreeing to this License, User represents to CCC and to such Publishers that it will conduct any sampling in compliance with the procedures agreed to by the parties. User also agrees to permit CCC to participate on its premises during sampling periods to the extent CCC feels it necessary to verify the accuracy of User's samples.

6. The Publishers listed in Schedule A have warranted that:

(a) during the first year of this license, and subject to User's adherence hereto, they will refrain from pursuing any unasserted claims of copyright infringement they may have arising from copying by User for internal use at any licensed facility of articles or chapters (or portions thereof) from any of the works licensed hereunder prior to the effective date of this license.; and

(b) should User elect to renew this license in accordance with Paragraph 8 hereof, and subject to User's adherence to this license, they will waive any unasserted claims of copyright infringement they may have arising from copying by User for internal use at any licensed facility of articles or chapters (or portions thereof) from any of the works licensed hereunder prior to the effective date of this license.

7. Except as this license may be modified as provided in Paragraph 10 hereof, this license pertains only to articles or chapters from the works listed in Schedule A and does not grant any rights to reproduce portions of any works not listed.

8. The period of this license is one year ("first annual license term"), commencing_____, and is automatically renewable for a one-year period ("renewal term"), at the election of the User. No later than 45 days prior to termination of the first annual license term, CCC shall notify User of the fees then in effect for the works listed in Schedule A as well as for such additional works as CCC will have become au-

thorized to license during the first annual license term, and of the total license fee determined in like manner as in the original Schedule B. User shall notify CCC, no later than 15 days prior to the expiration of the first annual license term, whether it elects to renew for the renewal term. No further sample of User's activities will be required in connection with the establishment of fees for such renewal term unless a change has taken place at the licensed premises that might reasonably be expected to have had a significant effect upon User's copying activities at said premises.

9. No later than 180 days prior to expiration of the renewal term, User shall notify CCC of its interest in further annual licenses (comprising a new first annual license term and, at User's option, a renewal term). The fees for such licenses will be determined on the basis of that standard CCC statistical and sampling procedure selected by User from among those then in effect and available to Users similarly situated to User. If such further licenses are desired, User agrees to cooperate with CCC in conducting any new sample in accordance with CCC's request. In advance of such expiration, CCC shall notify User of the license fees computed in accordance with the selected statistical and sampling procedure. User shall thereafter, and in no event later than 15 days prior to the expiration of the renewal term, inform CCC whether User wishes to enter into such further annual licenses. If User does not enter into such a further license, CCC shall advise each Publisher covered by the prior User License of User's withdrawal from the licensing system.

10. If during the period of this license or renewal thereof CCC becomes authorized to offer User Licenses covering additional works determined by any appropriate sample to have been copied by User, CCC shall periodically offer User amendments to cover the licensing of such works at appropriate additional fees.

11. CCC is authorized to act as agent of the Publishers in granting this license on the terms set forth herein.

12. CCC shall keep confidential and shall not disclose to Publishers or anyone else, except pursuant to court process or order, any of the information User supplies to it concerning specific User copying transactions except to the extent CCC is required to make disclosures pursuant to the following provision of CCC's agreements with Publishers:

"CCC shall report to Publisher at least semiannually information and data setting forth: (a) the identities of Users licensed hereunder; (b) the aggregate license fees payable to, as well as license fees actually collected by, CCC on Publisher's behalf with respect to each User; and

(c) the license fees payable to, as well as license fees actually collected by, CCC on Publisher's behalf from all Users in the aggregate with respect to each work subject to this Agreement.

Upon written request of Publisher, CCC shall additionally provide Publisher with information as to each User's aggregate annual copying volume of all works of all Publishers. CCC shall establish general ranges (in increments of no more than 10,000 pages per year and sufficient to include all Users) pertaining to the total numbers of pages copied by Users from the works of all participating publishers (based upon sample results) and CCC's reports to Publisher concerning the aggregate number of pages copied by any specific User shall be limited to disclosing the general range within which the User's copying falls. Publisher shall keep confidential and shall not disclose beyond its organization (unless required by court action or other government action or unless the information is, or becomes, part of the public domain through no fault of Publisher) information obtained from CCC in respect of User's copying activities. CCC shall not otherwise divulge any other information concerning any specific User's or other participating publisher's copying transactions, which shall be kept strictly confidential by CCC."

In the event of court process or order requiring production of information, CCC shall provide notification to User but shall not be required to actively oppose providing the information sought. CCC shall retain information concerning specific User copying transactions only for such time period as necessary to fulfill CCC's obligations to Publishers in respect of this licensing program. Such information thereafter shall be destroyed.

13. Neither party to this Agreement shall have the right to assign or sublicense any of its rights or obligations hereunder without the prior written consent of the other party.

14. This Agreement constitutes the entire agreement between the

parties with respect to the subject matter hereof and may not be modified or amended except in writing signed by the parties hereto.

15. This Agreement shall be interpreted, construed, governed and enforced in accordance with and under the laws of the State of New York, and any claims or disputes arising out of this Agreement shall be resolved by binding arbitration to be held in New York City in accordance with the Commercial Arbitration Association, and judgment upon the award rendered by the Arbitrator(s) may be entered in any court having jurisdiction thereof.

16. Publishers have warranted that they are authorized to license the rights granted herein. This license is given without any other warranty or recourse.

BIBLIOGRAPHY

American Library Association. *Comments of the American Library Association on the Report of the Register of Copyrights to Congress: Library Reproduction of Copyrighted Works (17 U.S.C. 108).* Washington, DC: ALA, 1983.

American Library Association. *Librarian's Guide to the New Copyright Law.* Chicago: ALA, 1977.

American Library Association. *Model Policy Concerning College and University Photocopying for Classroom Research and Library Reserve Use.* Chicago: ALA, 1982.

Bender, Ivan. "Copyright Law and Educational Media." *Library Trends* 34 (Summer 1985): 95–110.

Billings, Roger D., Jr. "Fair Use Under the 1976 Copyright Act: the Legacy of Williams & Wilkins for Librarians." *Library Trends* 32 (Fall, 1983): 183–198.

Copyright Clearance Center, Inc. *Handbook for Libraries and Other Organizational Users Which Copy from Serials and Separates: Procedures for Using the Programs of the Copyright Clearance Center, Inc.* New York: Copyright Clearance Center, Inc., 1977.

The Copyright Directory: Attorneys, Professors, Government Agencies, Congressional Committees, Searchers, Clearinghouses, Hotlines & Associations, 1990–91. Friday Harbor, WA: Copyright Information Services, Inc., 1990.

"Copyright Law Prompts New ILL Form." *American Libraries* 18 (October, 1987): 492-B, 492-C.

Copyright Law Revision Studies Pursuant to S. Res. 240, 86th Cong., 2nd Sess. (Comm. Print. 1960).

"The Gentlemen's Agreement and the Problem of Copyright." *Journal of Documentary Reproduction* 2 (1939): 29–36.

Heilprin, Laurence B., ed. *Copyright and Photocopying: Papers on Problems and Solutions, Design for a Clearinghouse, and a Bibliography.* College Park, MD: Univ. of Maryland, 1977.

Heller, James S. "Copyright and Fee-Based Copying Services." *College and Research Libraries* 47 (January 1986): 28–37.

Heller, James S. and Sarah K. Wiant. *Copyright Handbook*. Littleton, CO: American Association of Law Libraries, 1984.

Helm, Virginia. *What Educators Should Know About Copyright*. Bloomington, IN: Phi Delta Kappa Educational Foundation, 1986.

Hunter, Carolyn Owlett. "Library Reproduction of Musical Works: a Review of Revision." *Library Trends* 32 (Fall, 1983): 241–248.

Johnston, Donald F. *Copyright Handbook*, 2d ed. New York: R.R. Bowker, 1982.

Kaplan, Benjamin and Brown, Ralph S., Jr. *Cases on Copyright, Unfair Competition, and Other Topics Bearing on the Protection of Literary, Musical, and Artistic Works*, 3rd ed. Mineola, NY: The Foundation Press, 1978.

Lawrence, John Shelton and Bernard Timberg, eds. *Fair Use and Free Inquiry*. Norwood, NJ: Ablex Pub., 1980.

Matthews, Linda M. "Copyright and the Duplication of Personal Papers in Archival Repositories." *Library Trends* 32 (Fall, 1983): 223–240.

Miller, Jerome K. *Applying the New Copyright Law: a Guide for Educators & Librarians*. Chicago: American Library Assn., 1979.

Miller, Jerome K. *U.S. Copyright Documents: an Annotated Collection for Use by Educators and Librarians*. Littleton, CO: Libraries Unlimited, Inc., 1981.

Miller, Jerome K. *Using Copyrighted Videocassettes in Classrooms, Libraries, and Training Centers*, 2d ed. Friday Harbor, WA: Copyright Information Services, Inc., 1988.

National Commission on Libraries and Information Science *Library Photocopying in the United States, With Implications for the Development of a Copyright Royalty Payment Mechanism*. Prepared by King Research, Inc. Washington, DC: Government Printing Office, 1977.

The Official Fair Use Guidelines. 4th ed. Friday Harbor, WA: Copyright Information Services, Inc., 1989.

O'Leary, Mick. "The Information Broker: a Modern Profile." *Online* 11 (November 1987): 24–30.

Photocopy Services in ARL Libraries, SPEC #115, June, 1985.

Photocopying by Corporate Libraries. Prepared by the Association of American Publishers, Inc. and by the Authors League of America, Inc. Washington, DC: Association of American Publishers, 1978.

Putnam, George Haven, comp. *The Question of Copyright*. New York: Putnam, 1891.

Regan, Kathlene and Riordan, Virginia. "The Copyright Clearance Center: Growing Success in the United States Towards Increasing Copyright Protection of Print Publications." *Interlending and Document Supply* 16 (1988): 3–6.

Riordan, Virginia. "Copyright Clearance Center, 1988: a Progress Report." *Serials Librarian* 15, nos. 3/4 (1988): 43–54.

Seltzer, Leon E. *Exemptions and Fair Use in Copyright: the Exclusive Rights Tensions in the 1976 Copyright Act*. Cambridge, MA: Harvard Univ. Press, 1978.

Strong, William S. *The Copyright Book: a Practical Guide*. Cambridge, MA: MIT Press, 1990.

Talab, R. S. *Commonsense Copyright: a Guide to the New Technologies*. Jefferson, NC: McFarland & Co., Inc, 1986.

"Three Words Added to Copyright Notice" *American Libraries* 9 (January 1978): 22.

U.S. Library of Congress. Copyright Office. *Circular R1: Copyright Basics*. Washington, DC: Government Printing Office, 1988.

U.S. Library of Congress. Copyright Office. *Circular R21: Reproduction of Copyrighted Works by Educators and Librarians*. Washington, DC: Government Printing Office, 1978.

U.S. Library of Congress. Copyright Office. *Report of the Register of*

Copyrights: Library Reproduction of Copyrighted Works (17 U.S.C. 108). Washington, DC: January, 1983.

U.S. Library of Congress. Copyright Office. *Report of the Register of Copyrights: Library Reproduction of Copyrighted Works (17 U.S.C. 108)*. Washington, DC: January, 1988.

U.S. Library of Congress. Network Development and MARC Standards Office. *Intellectual Property Issues in the Library Network Context. Proceedings of the Library of Congress Network Advisory Committee Meeting, March 23–25, 1988*. Washington, DC: Government Printing Office, 1989.

University Copyright Policies in ARL Institutions, SPEC Flyer #138, October, 1987.

Vlcek, Charles W. *Adoptable Copyright Policy*. Washington, DC: Association for Educational Communications and Technology, Copyright Information Services, 1992.

Vlcek, Charles W. *Copyright Policy Development: a Resource Book for Educators*. Friday Harbor, WA: Copyright Information Services, Inc., 1987.

Warner, Alice Sizer. "Information Brokering: the State of the Art." *Wilson Library Bulletin* 63 (April, 1989): 55–57.

Warner, Alice Sizer. *Mind Your Own Business*. Chicago: Neal- Schuman Publishers, 1987.

"Warning Notices for Copies and Machines." *American Libraries* 8 (November, 1977): 530.

Warnken, Kelly and Felicetti, Barbara, eds. *So You Want to Be an Information Broker?* Chicago: Information Alternative, 1982.

White, Daniel H. "Annotation: Unauthorized Photocopying by Library as Infringement of Copyright." 21 A.L.R. Fed. 212.

Whitestone, Patricia. *Photocopying in Libraries: the Librarians Speak*. White Plains, NY: Knowledge Industry Publications, Inc., 1977.

Court Cases

Folsom v. Marsh, 9 Fed. Cas. 342, No. 4901 (C.C.D. Mass. 1841).

Williams & Wilkins Co. v. United States, 172 U.S.P.Q. 670 (Comm'r Ct. Cl. 1973), rev'd 487 F.2d 1345 (Ct. Cl. 1973) aff'd by an equally divided court, 420 U.S. 376 (1975).

Statutory References

U.S. Const., Art.I, Sec.1, cl.8.

Copyright Act of 1976, 17 U.S.C. 101 et seq. (effective 1/1/78).

37 C.F.R. 201.14

Congressional Reports

H.R. Rep. No. 2237, 89th Cong., 2d Sess., 1966

H.R. Rep. No. 83, 90th Cong., 1st Sess., 1967

Sen. Rep. No. 473, 94th Cong., 1st Sess., 1975

H.R. Rep. No. 1476, 94th Cong., 2d Sess., 1976

H.R. Rep. No. 1733, 94th Cong., 2d Sess., 1976 (Conf)

INDEX